THE BIG BOOK OF DYNAMICS AND GAMES FOR KIDS WITH AUTISM SPECTRUM DISORDER

115 Activities to work on emotions, social skills and other key skills

Maren Neely

Copyright © Maren Neely 2021

All Rights Reserved

INDEX

FOREWORD 7

DYNAMICS FOR WORKING ON VOCABULARY AND INCORRECT GRAMMATICAL STRUCTURES ... 15

GROUP DYNAMICS TO WORK ON EMOTIONS 20

GROUP DYNAMICS TO WORK ON SOCIAL SKILLS 25

GROUP DYNAMICS FOR MOTOR SKILLS WORK 34

GROUP DYNAMICS TO WORK ON RESISTANCE TO CHANGE 39

GROUP DYNAMICS TO WORK ON RIGIDITY 44

GROUP DYNAMICS TO WORK ON VERBAL COMMUNICATION 49

GROUP DYNAMICS TO WORK ON TRUST 54

GROUP DYNAMICS TO STIMULATE SIMULATION AND IMITATION ACTIVITIES. 59

GROUP DYNAMICS TO WORK WITH IMPULSIVITY 64

GROUP DYNAMICS TO WORK ON CREATIVITY 69

GROUP DYNAMICS TO WORK ON RULE ADHERENCE 74

GROUP DYNAMICS TO WORK ON TOLERANCE 80

GROUP DYNAMICS TO WORK ON NON-PRECISE LANGUAGE COMPREHENSION 85

GROUP DYNAMICS TO WORK ON THE DIFFICULTY OF ESTABLISHING EYE CONTACT WITH THE OTHER PERSON 90

GROUP DYNAMICS TO WORK ON INTROVERSION 96

GROUP DYNAMICS TO WORK ON OBSESSION WITH PARTICULAR OBJECTS OR THINGS 101

GROUP DYNAMICS TO WORK ON INTELLIGENCE DEVELOPMENT 108

GROUP DYNAMICS TO WORK ON SELF-ESTEEM 113

GROUP DYNAMICS FOR WORKING ON SENSITIVITY TO DIFFERENT SENSORY STIMULI 119

GROUP DYNAMICS TO WORK ON THE ABILITY TO ACCEPT THE AFFECTION AND SUPPORT OF OTHERS 124

GROUP DYNAMICS TO WORK ON THE DIFFICULTY OF REPEATING PHRASES, WORDS OR SOUNDS IN A CONSECUTIVE WAY 129

GROUP DYNAMICS TO WORK ON THE DEVELOPMENT OF SKILLS TO GIVE ASSERTIVE ANSWERS TO THE QUESTIONS ASKED 134

GROUP DYNAMICS TO WORK ON ANGER 139

GROUP DYNAMICS FOR WORKING ON UNDERSTANDING THE LIMITS OF PERSONAL SPACE 146

GROUP DYNAMICS TO WORK ON THE NEED TO BE ALONE 151

GROUP DYNAMICS TO WORK ON THE USE OF THE DIFFERENT MEANS OF COMMUNICATION IN AN APPROPRIATE WAY 156

FOREWORD

Autism spectrum disorder is a condition related to brain development, which affects the way a person perceives and relates to others, resulting in conflicts in communication and social interaction.

This neurodevelopmental disorder has a neurobiological origin and begins in childhood, with the presence of restricted and repetitive behaviors and interests, its evolution is chronic, affecting in different degrees the functional adaptation, language functioning and intellectual development, depending on the case and its development.

The definition and diagnosis of Autism, also called ASD, has undergone certain modifications and adaptations in recent years, as a result of a series of investigations.

The DSM-5 (Diagnostic and Statistical Manual of Mental Disorders of the American Psychiatric Association) introduces a generic denomination of ASD and excludes the subcategories that had been presented in the DSM-4, thus giving a dimensional concept of autism.

With its publication and new criteria in the autism area, the classification of autism was considerably modified.

The different autism spectrum disorders in the DSM-4, autistic disorder, Asperger syndrome and pervasive developmental disorder not otherwise specified, among others, were eliminated to be included in a single nomenclature of autism spectrum disorders ASD.

Psychiatrist Kanner Leo (1943) described autistic disorder as lack of contact with people, self-absorption and emotional loneliness. He wasn't the first physician to perceive the symptoms, but he was the first to differentiate it from schizophrenia.

General symptoms of autism in children

In some cases, children show signs of autism in early childhood, they have difficulty establishing eye contact, giving answers when called by name or apathy with caregivers.

Others may develop normally in the first months or years of life, but then unexpectedly become withdrawn, introverted, aggressive or lose language skills they had achieved. Signs usually appear after the age of two.

There is a percentage of children with ASD who have learning difficulties, while others have signs of intelligence that are considered below normal.

However, in particular cases a normal to high intelligence can be perceived, they learn very fast, although they have some difficulty to communicate, to be able to apply their knowledge and to adapt to different social environments.

Perhaps autism spectrum disorders have a pattern of behavior and a level of severity that is considered unique in each case, which can range from very low to very high functioning.

Depending on the unique symptoms that characterize each child, it is sometimes very difficult to discriminate the level of severity, usually taken as a reference point the level of impairment and how it affects the ability to perform adequately in different contexts in what makes life.

There are different cases, however, when they are known exactly, different strategies and tools can be found to improve relationships with them and incorporate them into different contexts without major inconvenience.

Children with this condition are often incorporated without an accurate diagnosis in different areas and routines, which results in many of them feeling frustrated and misunderstood.

It is necessary to provide tools to all the people involved in their environment, so that they can treat them in a timely manner and relate to them, creating an environment of trust and empathy.

A child with ASD will hardly be open to share or establish interpersonal relationships with those he/she does not know or is not close to, on the contrary, a child who knows his/her routine and all the people involved, will more easily be able to open up to the experience of knowing and being known.

In this way, little by little, he/she will begin a process of integration that, in the long term, will bring great benefits in many areas of development.

Symptoms in communication and social relationships

Children with ASD may have problems with social interaction and communication skills, which may present as follows:

- They do not respond when called by name, they do not seem to hear the call.

- They are closed with emotional expressions, so they do not respond to hugs, caresses or other forms of affective manifestations, it is assumed that they like solitude and prefer to withdraw into their own world.

- They do not express themselves with words, they do not talk much or they lose the capacity they had to communicate.

- It is not possible for them to initiate a communicative process and if they do it is only to ask for something.

- His speech and tone is abnormal, sometimes he speaks with a singsong voice or like a robot.

- He does not clearly understand the proper use of words, so he repeats phrases verbatim or words.

- Does not have the ability to express feelings and emotions, does not seem to understand or care about those of others.

- The use of objects to share interests is unknown.

- Approaches situations or social gatherings in a disruptive, inappropriate, passive or aggressive manner.

- Difficulty recognizing nonverbal expressions, such as facial interpretations in others.

- Inconvenience in repeating messages, words or sounds.

- They do not give correct answers when asked a question.

Behavior patterns

Generally, the behavior pattern in children with autism is repetitive and limited, even though each one has his particular interests, in each case the signs mentioned below may be present:

- Their movements are repetitive, such as rocking, spinning or hand flapping.

- They engage in activities that may unintentionally cause them harm, such as head banging or biting.

- His routines or rituals are specific, if any change is made to them, they are altered.

- Presents coordination problems and strange movements, such as being clumsy or wanting to walk on tiptoe.

- Their body language is strange, rigid and strange.

- They are impressed by the details of objects, especially the wheels that turn in toy cars, even though they do not understand how it works.

- It is sensitive to physical contact, loud noises and light.

- He tends to be indifferent to heat or temperature.

- Does not participate in activities that require imitation or simulation.

- Is obsessive, out of the ordinary, with certain objects or activities.

- Presents special preferences in relation to foods to eat and exclude from their diet, or not eat others because they do not like their texture.

As they mature, autistic children begin to socialize with some people and show fewer alterations in their behavioral patterns.

Less severe cases may begin to live a more normal or near-normal life, however, there is another group that continues to present difficulties with language and social skills.

Causes of autism

Autism spectrum disorders do not have a defined cause, taking into consideration the complexity of the disorder and the fact that symptoms and severity vary in each case, there are possibly many causes, genetics and environment cannot be excluded.

In relation to genetics, it appears that several genes are associated with ASD, in some cases they may be linked to a genetic disorder, such as Rett syndrome or Fragile X syndrome.

Genes can affect brain development or the way in which brain neurons communicate, some mutations are inherited and others develop spontaneously.

As for environmental factors, many researchers are currently studying whether viral infections, medications, pregnancy complications or air pollutants play a role in the development of autism spectrum disorder.

How to live with a child with ASD?

Living with a child diagnosed with ASD is not easy, however, by using different tools and strategies, it is possible to have a harmonious, empathetic and trusting relationship, which will make him/her feel safe and loved.

You can make use of visual aids such as calendars or pictograms, maintain a calm and well-structured environment, and have a day-to-day order that allows him/her to acquire meaningful learning in a familiar environment.

If there is going to be any change in his daily routine, anticipate it, in order to initiate an adaptation process that does not alter his behavior.

Offer help when necessary, dividing complex tasks into small, simple activities to avoid episodes of frustration.

It is important to reinforce them positively to encourage learning and repetition of correct behaviors using modification techniques.

They should not be over stimulated, it is necessary to give them their space to rest, likewise they should not be overprotected, this generates independence to perform certain tasks by themselves.

It is possible to open spaces of motivation with their own interests and tastes, to develop new learning.

Work on patience and calmness to help them manage their emotions, especially explosions of anger and tantrums.

We must be aware that they are not to blame for what happens, they just have difficulties to manage and understand their emotions, for that reason, they should be given all possible support to help them to know themselves and their environment.

It is essential to focus on the present, on their small daily achievements and congratulate them for what, in the midst of their difficulty, they can achieve, it is a way to keep them motivated, they are not different, they just have a condition that makes them special and unique.

Group dynamics for working with children with autism

ASD is a disorder that causes alterations in the ability of children to relate and interact with others, thus restricting their interests and activities.

It has no cure, however, as the years go by, a considerable improvement in the symptoms can be perceived, in fact, it is considered that the earlier the treatment is started, the better the prognosis may be as the child grows up.

For this reason, specialists recommend working on a series of activities and training games, especially aimed at them to develop their skills, abilities and increase their capacities.

Group dynamics are an effective tool for the achievement of the proposed objective.

DYNAMICS FOR WORKING ON VOCABULARY AND INCORRECT GRAMMATICAL STRUCTURES

1- Letter game

Materials needed for this dynamic: Cardboard, numbers on cardboard, packaging.

Duration: approximately 20 minutes

Number of children: between 5 and 15 people

In general, children diagnosed with ASD have difficulty with vocabulary, as it is usually very poor and prevents them from communicating easily.

They also find it difficult to understand other people's vocabulary, especially if they are asked questions, given instructions or if they are simply joking.

The dynamic consists of taking the cardboard and placing different letters, in turn, the cardboard letters, which have to be prepared beforehand, must be introduced into the container.

The letters on the cardboard must coincide with those found in the container, the dynamic will consist of each of the children finding the letters on the cardboard to make them coincide.

Each time a participant finds a letter, he/she must pronounce it and repeat the sound, and so on until he/she has found all the letters on the cardboard and is familiar with them.

2- Treasure hunt

Materials needed for this dynamic: Letters and words drawn on poster board.

Duration: 20 minutes

Number of children: between 5 to 15 people

The dynamic consists of drawing with the children a number of letters and words on cardboard, while drawing and coloring they must pronounce them, so that the significant learning that we want to achieve begins.

Once this first part is finished, the letters and words are taken and cut out, the leader who carries out the dynamics will be in charge of hiding them in ideal spaces in the place where they are located.

Once they are all hidden, the leader will tell the children that they must start the treasure hunt, everyone must start looking for them and when they find them they will let the children know that they have obtained part of the treasure.

For example, if one of the words is "magic", they will say I found the treasure "magic", I found the treasure "B", I found the treasure "one", and in this way the dynamics will develop until they find all the letters and words.

When they have found and identified all of them, they will gather them and proceed to mention them again one by one, out loud, thus concluding the dynamic.

Repeating the words over and over again will allow them to memorize them and enrich their vocabulary.

3- Playing with numbers

Materials needed for this dynamic: pencils, markers, wooden paddles, buttons, cardboard boxes.

Duration: approximately 30 to 45 minutes

Number of children: 5 to 15 people

Children with autism find it very attractive to play with numbers, although it is often difficult for them to understand the logic of calculations, they are entertained and attracted by lining up objects or always playing with the same quantity.

The dynamic starts by collecting all the useful and simple objects that allow the development of the same, all of them have to be placed in combination with each other.

Once all the objects have been located, the children are asked, one by one, to take a specific quantity of them and put them in the appropriate box.

The intention is that they organize them according to their classification, pencils with pencils, palettes with palettes, markers with markers, buttons with buttons.

When they finish organizing them all, they take the boxes and begin to count them one by one, establishing differences in their shape, color or kind.

4- I listen and understand

Materials needed for this dynamic: sheet and paper

Duration: 20 minutes

Number of children: between 5 and 15 people

One of the great conflicts of a child with autism is to be able to relate to others through a communicative process, most of them tend to ignore conversations, instructions and questions, either because they are unable to understand or because of lack of interest.

This is one of the aspects that deserves more attention, since their communication and independence in their environment will largely depend on it.

The dynamic consists of calling the child's attention, either by touching him or calling his name.

The objective is for the child to become familiar with paying attention every time a call is made. This can be repeated several times, then start transmitting a message slowly and clearly.

Example, take the pencil and after you have it in your hand, write on your sheet your name.

Once everyone has done, we then proceed to formulate more structured sentences, using paraphrasing and redundancy, and at the end we ask if they understood the message and ask them to reproduce it.

This action will reinforce learning and help them develop their attention span when called upon or given instructions.

GROUP DYNAMICS TO WORK ON EMOTIONS

5- What emotion is it?

Materials needed for this dynamic: pictograms or cards with different gestures of emotions.

Duration: 40 minutes

Number of children: between 5 and 15 people

Children with ASD usually have difficulty expressing emotions as well as receiving them from others, for this reason, it is necessary to incorporate certain activities that help them to recognize and manage them.

The person in charge of leading the group will stand in front of each child with a card that identifies an emotion: joy, sadness, anger, rage, among others.

Each time an emotion is placed in front of the child, it will be explained what it is, so that the child can recognize it and understand it by observing the image.

It is important to describe it in detail, as well as their facial features, when they have been shown all of them then the roles will be reversed.

The child will be in charge of taking the cards, showing them and explaining which emotion each one is related to.

Finally, the pictogram or the cards are shown one by one without saying a word so that the child can identify them and call them by name.

6- How do I feel?

Materials needed for this dynamic: pictograms or cards with drawings of emotions.

Duration: 30 minutes

Number of children: between 5 and 15 people

The dynamic consists of telling the children about an event that has awakened some emotion, love, sadness, joy, anger, rage, anger, among others.

Then, some of the children will be asked to participate, in which they can also express an experience where they have experienced emotions.

When everyone completes their participation, the pictogram is taken and the group begins to relate each image with the emotions exposed.

The first to participate will be the group leader, looking for the image that represents what he/she said.

This will give way to the participation of each of those who expressed themselves so that with the pictogram they can identify what they felt in the action they narrated.

This activity will help them to recognize what they feel at a certain moment that is so difficult for them to understand.

7- We build a traffic light

Materials needed for this dynamic: black cardboard, scissors, markers, glue, plastic tape.

Duration: 30 minutes

Number of children: between 5 and 15 people

A red circle, a yellow circle and a green circle will be placed on the black cardboard. A black cross will also be made with plastic tape on the back so that it can be glued when needed, depending on the mood of each child.

The traffic light will allow them to identify how they feel at a certain moment, then we will proceed to explain the meaning of each color, red represents stop, when they cannot stop or control their emotions.

Yellow is the moment to become aware that it is time to think and rethink about what is happening and has led them to stop in the red color.

Green represents the moment to look for the solution offered, so it is time to reflect.

The children are told a story in which different emotions are present and then they are asked to place the black arrow in the color they think it should be, because of what the experience makes them feel.

Once they have placed their arrows, we talk to them about the importance of learning to stop in the color red to think about the possible solutions that can be given to the different situations that arise in everyday life.

8- We read a book story

Materials needed for this dynamic: book

Duration: 30 minutes

Number of children: between 5 and 15 person

This dynamic is very simple, it consists of reading a story to the group of children in which different emotions are present, they should listen carefully so that no detail escapes them.

When the reading is finished, a question and answer session will be opened in which the children will be able to participate and explain what they understood by explaining the emotions they were able to identify.

In addition, they will have the opportunity to put themselves in the other person's place, this is very important because they will understand that others are also capable of expressing and receiving emotions.

To conclude the dynamic, a small and simple reflection is made in which they can conceive that emotions are natural in human beings, and that for this reason it is necessary to learn about them in themselves and in others for a better coexistence.

GROUP DYNAMICS TO WORK ON SOCIAL SKILLS

9- Hidden

Materials needed for this dynamic: whistle

Duration: 30 minutes

Number of children: between 5 and 15 people

Children diagnosed with ASD present a great conflict when it comes to establishing interpersonal relationships with others. In general, they are always isolated and it is not because they want to be, but because including themselves in certain activities generates stress for them because they lack tools.

A child is selected who can count while the others find a place to hide.

When everyone is located and safe, the counting child will say "I'm coming for you," and the search will begin.

The idea is that everyone manages to mislead the searcher so that they can get home safely. If the child doing the search finds them before they can get home, then they will lose and leave the game.

The ideal is that together they can find a way to save themselves before they are found.

Many of them will know each other's hiding place, so they can alert them with the whistle if they see the searching child nearby.

Being able to help protect each other will encourage companionship and socialization with their peers.

10- Pilla pilla

Materials needed for this dynamic: letters and words drawn on poster board.

Duration: 20 minutes

Number of children: between 5 and 15 persons

A space must be delimited for the protection of the children, this will be their safe place and no one will be able to touch them.

One child will be selected and will be in charge of chasing them through all the spaces until they are caught.

The rest of the children will be able to move freely in the area destined for the dynamic, but only in the delimited space they will be protected.

The dynamic begins and everyone will have to move avoiding the child who wants to touch him, if he succeeds, the touched child will take his place and start chasing the rest of the children.

If, on the contrary, he/she does not manage to make contact and the other child enters the delimited area, he/she will be safe.

This action will be repeated for a short period of time until everyone has gained confidence and between shouts and laughter can understand that interacting with others is a fundamental need of human beings on a daily basis.

11- The handkerchief

Materials needed for this dynamic: a handkerchief

Duration: 30 minutes

Number of children: between 5 and 15

The group of children is divided into two teams, and one team is selected to be in charge of leading the dynamic.

A line is drawn in the center of the space, and the teams are placed side by side.

Each member will have a different number that identifies him/her. The child who will lead the dynamic stand just above the line with a handkerchief in hand and will mention a number out loud.

The childrens of the different teams will run, the first one to take the handkerchief will be the winner and add points for his/her group.

The team that gets the most correct numbers will be the winner, the emphasis will be on the importance of working together to achieve positive results and socialize with their peers.

12- The wolf and the sheep

Materials needed for this dynamic: colored handkerchiefs

Duration: 20 minutes

Number of children: between 5 and 15

A space is taken and delimited; it will be the place of protection for each of the children who participate in the dynamics.

One child will be in charge of representing the wolf and the rest will represent the sheep. The sheep will be safe in their place of protection, but if they are found by the wolf and there is no one to help them, they will be out of the game.

However, they will be identified with colored handkerchiefs, two red, two green, two blue and so on, if the wolf catches one of them and its colored partner comes to its aid, the wolf must release it and let it go.

This is how the dynamic will develop until the wolf defeats the sheep or the sheep defeat the wolf.

The main objective is to promote teamwork and the importance of reinforcing the interrelationship with other persons.

Regardless of the circumstances, human beings are not isolated beings and require the support and companionship of others.

13- Guess the gesture

Duration: 30 minutes

Number of children: between 5 and 15 people

A large circle is made with all the children who participate in the dynamic, and the dynamic begins freely making expressions with certain gestures, which are shown in the pictogram, explaining what is meant by each one and why they are often used in the communicative process.

Then an experience is told, making use of them again, but this time they are asked to identify them.

Now the children are asked to express some action, feeling or emotion, without using words, and the rest of the children are asked to guess.

In this way, the action will be repeated until everyone is familiar with the dynamics and is able to understand what is being expressed.

This activity helps the development of the child's thinking, allowing him/her to understand that there are many forms of expression and that he/she should be open to all of them, since they contribute to improve interpersonal relationships with the environment on a daily basis.

It is not a strange or unknown language, but a different one, from which we also learn and enrich our vocabulary.

14- Observing I learn

Materials needed for this dynamic: sheet of bond paper, markers.

Duration: 30 minutes

Number of children: between 5 and 15 people

Children are invited to sit in pairs and are given markers and bond paper.

When everyone is organized, the reading of a story begins, which will be full of emotions that will be represented by the person reading.

The children will listen attentively and will have the task of drawing each gesture expressed by the person reading and those that they consider appear in the story while they listen until the end.

At the end, each pair will take the floor to summarize what they have understood and will emphasize each of the gestures they heard, observed and were able to draw, explaining the meaning of each one at the same time.

With this dynamic it is intended that the child with ASD can open up to this type of communication acquiring tools that will allow him/her a better development in his/her environment.

15- Represent the image

Materials needed for this dynamic: cards or pictograms

Duration: 400 minutes

Number of children: between 5 and 15 people

The dynamic will begin by talking about non-verbal communication and the importance of understanding it for an optimal coexistence.

Then, the cards will be taken and the children will be shown the images represented there, explaining the meaning of each one.

Once everyone has the information clear, they will proceed to give a card to each one and ask them to represent the image they have been given.

While they represent the image, the rest of the group has the task of guessing the gesture that the other person makes and explaining what he/she wants to transmit.

Everyone will have the opportunity to participate, which will allow a greater understanding of the dynamics and what is to be transmitted, thus contributing to the development of the ability of children with ASD to understand this form of language.

16 - What do I want to say?

Materials needed for this dynamic: pencil and paper

Duration: 30 minutes

Number of children: between 5 and 15 people

With this activity the child will have the possibility, through clear observation, to understand the information expressed through non-verbal language.

The children will be placed in pairs and will be given a piece of paper with a message, which they will have to talk to each other, interpret and write on their paper.

Once they have finished this first part, they will have the possibility to express the assigned information to the rest of the group through gestures and signs.

Everyone will be able to participate, both in the transmission of their message and in guessing the message of the rest of the group.

This is a very practical dynamic that allows understand the different forms of communication without the need to utter words.

By applying these dynamics, the child with ASD will mature and when he/she finds himself in a situation that deserves his attention, will be open to receive what wants to express.

GROUP DYNAMICS FOR MOTOR SKILLS WORK

17- Balance

Materials needed for this dynamic: yarn

Duration: 20 minutes

Number of children: between 5 and 15 people

Activities for the development of both fine and gross motor skills are essential for children with ASD.

In general, it is difficult for them to perform such exercises involving physical activity, which can generate a feeling of frustration and inability.

The dynamics of balance consists of dividing the group into two teams, with the stamen a line is placed on the floor.

Each group will be from end to end, one by one will have the opportunity to move to the opposite side, over the yarn, balancing, when they arrive they will be waiting with a question of routine, sport, education, fashion, cooking, among others.

If you answer correctly, you will add points to your team, the one with the most points will be the winner.

Your active participation will improve the motor skills of the child with ASD.

18- Grab the ball and answer the question.

Materials needed for this dynamic: ball

Duration: 30 minutes

Number of children: between 5 and 15 people

The children will stand in a circle and initiate a guided but natural conversation about a specific topic that is of interest to all.

At the end of the conversation, a question and answer session will be opened in which everyone can participate.

The dynamic consists of passing the ball one by one, each one can throw it if he/she wishes to throw it to the partner of his/her choice.

When the person in charge of the group says "catch the ball and answer the question," the ball must remain in the hands it was in when the order was given.

A question is then asked, related to the topic of the initial conversation, which the child must answer.

Once everyone has participated, the closing is done, emphasizing the importance of cultivating physical activities for a better development.

19- Jump while you can

Materials needed for this dynamic: colored tape

Duration: 30 minutes

Number of children: between 5 and 15 people

The children will be placed in pairs and in their hand they will wear a colored ribbon that identifies them, i.e., a red pair, a green pair, a blue pair, and so on.

One of the children will be placed at the end of the space where they are against the wall, the rest of the children will be at the other end.

When the child against the wall begins to count, everyone must quickly move forward, as far as they can.

When they turn around they must all remain still, the child who is counting will stand in front and try to make them move, if he succeeds they will lose and must retreat.

However, as they are identified in pairs, the other child with the same color will continue the game, and if they reach the goal, both will win.

If, on the other hand, both are eliminated, then they must withdraw from the game. The child or pair that manages to reach the front after each count will win.

This activity, like the previous ones, is ideal for improving motor skills in children with ASD.

20- The plane is going to land

Duration: 20 minutes

Number of children: between 5 and 15 people

The simulation challenge is a considerable case in children with autism, as they can benefit from the movements while their imagination is also at work.

The group of children will be placed in the place of their choice, the dynamics will consist in that they will have to start simulating, with their arms open, that the airplane flies all over the space.

When they hear, from the voice of the person who carries out the dynamic: "the plane is going to land," they must lower their wings and remain still.

The person who gave the stop signal will stand in front of them in order to make them move, so that they lose.

The child who manages to remain still will continue active in the activity, the one who moved, will not leave the space, but will remain in the same place until the activity is over.

With each immobile child, the one who is in movement will find it more complex to develop with freedom and open arms in the place.

This will help to improve them, thus developing their motor skills.

GROUP DYNAMICS TO WORK ON RESISTANCE TO CHANGE

21- Change of place

Materials needed for this dynamic: book

Duration: 20 minutes

Number of children: between 5 and 15 people

Children diagnosed with autism tend to have a fairly rigid routine, so they often resist change.

They love to follow the same activities every day and get angry very easily if a different signal is given to them, without having anticipated it.

The children will be seated each one in a chair, the person in charge of carrying out the dynamic will start a reading and will explain that every time there is a pause, they will have to stand up and change chairs.

This is how the activity will start, the reading begins and everyone listens attentively, when everything is silent, they will stand up and change chairs with each other.

They do not necessarily have to sit in the chair on the side, it can be the one in the back or the one in the front, when the reading resumes, everyone must be in their place.

If anyone is left standing, he/she will lose the game and have to retire, the winner will be the one who manages to finish sitting down.

It is possible that at the beginning the child with ASD may feel a little confused, but as he/she becomes familiar with the activity, he/she will understand that the changes are part of everyday life.

22- Find the object

Materials needed for this dynamic: buttons, pencils, markers, books.

Duration: 30 – 40 minutes

Number of children: 5 to 15

Different objects are taken and placed in separate spaces, the children should observe each one and the place where they are located.

Then they are placed in a circle and begin to sing and play with each other as they wish, while the person who directs them changes the objects.

After a short time, he/she will tell them "let's look for the pencils," the first action will be to go to the main place where they had been kept.

If they do not find them there, they will have the challenge of going through all the spaces until they find them.

When they hear again "let's look for the buttons," they will start the search again, but this time they will understand that the objects may be in another place and they will search little by little.

The idea is to emphasize the changes and daily routines so that they can understand that they are a natural part of daily life.

23- Change the message

Duration: 30 minutes

Number of children: between 5 and 15 people

The children will form two rows, one next to the other. The person who directs them will proceed to give information in the ear to the first ones in each row and will indicate that they must transmit it to the rest, but with their own words.

Start the dynamic and one by one pass the message, first say it out loud and then proceed to make changes, but without changing the intention of the message.

The idea is that while they listen they can formulate the possible changes that correspond to the message.

At the end, they will have the task of verifying if what they expressed, really keeps the essence of the first message given.

A space will be opened in which they can expose what generated them to think about the transformation they had to make and if it cost them a lot of work.

Emphasizing the importance of adapting to all those situations that arise in the daily routine, often altering the planned tasks.

24- Time out

Duration: 30 – 40 minutes

Number of children: between 5 and 15 people

The children should form small groups of three to four people, one of them will be in charge of reading, while the others listen attentively.

The dynamics will consist in that while they read, they will be given certain spaces to make changes.

When the person in charge of leading the dynamic says "time out", quickly, the child who is reading must change groups and start reading again.

This will be done successively until all the children have rotated through the different groups.

You can also make changes among the children doing the reading to give everyone a chance to participate.

It will be a fun experience and while they learn, they will understand that changes, no matter how small they may seem, are present in every routine and the best way to adapt to them is to recognize and accept them.

GROUP DYNAMICS TO WORK ON RIGIDITY

25- Jump rope and recover the object

Materials needed for this dynamic: ropes, objects such as pencils, buttons, ornaments, etc.

Duration: 30 minutes

Number of children: between 5 and 15 people

Generally, children with ASD tend to have a very rigid behavior in their body language, so they are often considered strange.

It is not abnormal, it is their way of being, but being able to show them that there are different forms of expression can help them to understand their environment better and to make certain modifications in the way they also express themselves bodily.

The person in charge of developing the dynamic will distribute the space so that it can develop assertively and correctly.

In specific spaces, he/she will place all the objects that can be used; it is suggested to use corners and centers. The rope will be in the center of the place.

Then, invite the children to form two groups, they will be entertained playing, singing, laughing, when they hear "jump rope and retrieve the object," they should run to where the rope is, the first one to take it, jumping with it, will go to one of the spaces and retrieve the object that is there, bringing it to his group.

The dynamic will be repeated as many times as necessary and all the objects are recovered, the team with the highest number of objects will be the winner.

While the same is developed, some will shout, others will jump, others will laugh, at the end it should be mentioned that all the actions developed corporally are also an important part of the way in which the human being communicates and transmits emotions.

26- Change of partner

Materials needed for this dynamic: music player

Duration: 30 minutes

Number of children: between 5 and 15

Dancing is one of the best known forms of corporal expression, besides being a way to release stress and exhaustion due to some routine.

The children will be placed in pairs to dance, perhaps many are not given to dance, however, the music used should be one that allows them to move and make free movements.

It will play for a few minutes and then it will be indicated that they should change partners.

They will be placed with their new partner and will start dancing again, and this will be done for a period of time that will be of great entertainment for them.

To end the dynamic, they will make a big circle in which everyone can make free movements, while the music continues to play.

They are told how much fun it is to be able to express themselves bodily and if they wish to express how they felt, a space is opened for participation.

27- Color - color

Materials needed for this dynamic: cards and colored chalk

Duration: 30 minutes

Number of children: between 5 and 15

A space is selected in the place where they are, with the colored chalks they will draw a board on the floor.

The children will place themselves around it, the person who directs the dynamic will be in front with the colored cards in their hands.

He/she will indicate to the children that a series of questions will be asked, the one who wants to answer must go to the board and place himself/herself on the color indicated by showing the color of the card.

For example, if a blue card is drawn, the child should place himself on the board in the blue color to answer.

Their response should be accompanied by an emotion or action, laughter, singing, jumping, hugging, hands up, whatever the child wishes.

When everyone has participated, the dynamic will be concluded by collecting their experiences and how they felt while expressing themselves using body language, remembering its importance in every communicative process.

28- Tell the joke

Duration: 30 minutes

Number of children: between 5 and 15 people

The children will be asked to sit in a circle, and the person leading the dynamic will start, as an example, to tell a joke with a lot of laughter.

Then, they will be given the instructions, for a few minutes they must think of some action, fact or joke that causes them a lot of fun, if they wish they can help each other.

At the beginning of the dynamic, they will be given the opportunity to come to the front to tell what each one planned, in their story they should incorporate laughter, in the way they want.

Generally, laughter is contagious, so it is likely that someone may not even be able to speak while laughing and infecting the others.

When a reasonable amount of time has passed, your director will take the floor to finish, but not before hearing how much fun the experience was, in which stiffness probably had to be set aside.

GROUP DYNAMICS TO WORK ON VERBAL COMMUNICATION

29- I talk, you explain

Materials needed for this dynamic: pencil and paper

Duration: 30 minutes

Number of children: between 5 and 15 persons

Children with ASD are very quiet and reserved, it is very difficult for them to establish communicative relationships with others.

It is not a question of not wanting to, but of a lack of tools and strategies that help them to forge relationships and express themselves freely.

The person leading the exercise will tell the children to get into pairs.

They should select a topic of conversation that they find pleasant and enjoyable, they both have to know about it so that they can have an assertive participation, if they wish they can write down some important elements.

Once they agree, they will come to the front to talk to the rest of the children about their topic of interest.

One will be in charge of speaking or reading and then the other will explain in their own different words what they both want to convey.

This is an opportune way for the child with ASD to participate and open up to express himself verbally, as this will help him to develop better in his environment, thus improving interpersonal relationships.

30- Follow her

Materials needed for this dynamic: children only

Duration: 30 minutes

Number of children: between 5 and 15 people

The children should be placed in a circle, the person leading the dynamic will give a message in the ear of each child and he/she in turn must reproduce it to his/her partner.

The message must pass through everyone, each one will have the opportunity to listen and structure it in the way he/she has understood it.

One by one the information will be passed on until it arrives again at the beginning.

The last one to receive it should say it out loud to verify that it arrived exactly as it came out.

It is possible that it has undergone some modifications, however, the importance lies in the fact that the child with ASD will have the opportunity not only to structure it, but also to express it verbally, thus enriching his verbal communication.

31- Repeat the message

Materials needed for this dynamic: children only

Duration: 30 minutes

Number of children: between 5 and 15 people

The group will be organized in pairs, one child should stand in front of the other, keeping a safe distance.

The leader of the group will pass them a message written on a piece of paper, only one of the members of the pair will receive it and will be in charge of reading it.

He/she will proceed to read it to the other partner in a soft tone of voice, so that he/she will make an effort to listen to it and can repeat it.

At the end of their participation, they will give way to the participation of the other child, who will have to repeat the message that was expressed in their own words.

Then they will exchange roles, the one who had listened first will be in charge of reading the message and the other one will have to reproduce it, in this way everyone will have participated and used oral language as a means of expression.

32- A letter arrived

Materials needed for this dynamic: paper and pencil, cardboard box.

Duration: 30 minutes

Number of children: between 5 and 15 people

All the children will be seated with their pencil and paper. The person in charge of carrying out the exercise will tell them that they must write a letter to another member of the group with whom they have the best relationship.

Once they have finished, they will all be placed in the cardboard box, the children will be seated in a circle and the box in the center.

The person leading the exercise will stand in the middle of the circle and indicate that a card has arrived.

He or she will select one of the children and pass him or her to the front, who will be in charge of taking one of the letters and reading it aloud to the person to whom the letter is dedicated.

At the end, he/she will return to his/her space, and so on, until all the children have participated and expressed themselves verbally.

This type of activity enriches the vocabulary of the children, providing them with tools that allow them to establish communicative situations with others.

GROUP DYNAMICS TO WORK ON TRUST

33- I create a story

Materials needed for this dynamic: sheets of paper, pencils, colors, markers, glue.

Duration: 30 – 40 minutes

Number of children: between 5 and 15 people

Children who are diagnosed with ASD are generally very insecure, which makes it difficult for them to establish trusting and empathetic relationships with others.

However, by providing them with the necessary tools, they can open up to a better relationship of trust with others, improving their interpersonal relationships.

The person in charge of developing the dynamics will place the children in pairs and will indicate that they must write a story, which must be created by themselves, so before starting to write they must exchange certain information related to the tastes of each one.

By sharing and getting to know their personal interests, they will have a better chance of finding similar elements in the writing of their story.

At the end, they will come to the front of the group and explain the process of creating their story and in their own words what it is about.

Since it is a topic of common interest, both will be able to participate without reading.

This will encourage the need to share in empathy and trust with the other, in order to achieve certain objectives.

34- The spider's web

Materials needed for this dynamic: yarn

Duration: 30 minutes

Number of children: between 5 and 15 people

The children should sit in a circle, with a roll of yarn in the hand of the person leading the dynamic, who will be in charge of starting the activity.

She takes the roll in her hand and says her name, something she likes, takes the end and throws the roll to one of the children sitting in the group.

Example, my name is Maria and I like to dance, the child who takes the roll in her hand, will follow the round, say her name, something she likes, take the tip and throw the roll to another participant.

The dynamics will be repeated until everyone has participated. At the end, it will be noticed that while passing the yarn from side to side, a large spider's web was formed.

The meaning of the spider web will be explained to the children, sometimes the human being fosters relationships that are like a spider web, very united and difficult to undo.

This type of relationships are not negative, on the contrary, being able to relate with trust and unity with the other, brings great benefits to the development of the personality, as well as a better development in the different tasks to be done in the day to day.

35- Holding hands

Materials needed for this dynamic: objects, pencils, markers, toys, etc.

Duration: 30 minutes

Number of children: between 5 and 15 people

The objects that are at hand will be distributed throughout the space where they are doing the dynamic, pencils, markers, toys, others.

Then, all the children will be placed in pairs, the work to be done must be done together, holding hands.

They will be placed at one end of the room or place, at the other end, when they reach the wall, will be the goal.

Together they must cross from one place to another, picking up all the obstacles that prevent them from moving, but they must do it holding hands, under no circumstances can they let go, if they do, they are disqualified and leave the game.

The first couple to arrive will be the winner. To finish, explain the importance of trusting each other to handle certain situations and open a space for interaction in which they can express how they felt and what they think about working as a team, placing their trust in the person who accompanies them.

36- We make necklaces

Materials needed for this dynamic: onion or crepe paper, glue, scissors.

Duration: 30 minutes

Number of children: between 5 and 15

The person leading the group will tell the children to get into pairs, and they will be given a sheet of onion or crepe paper, scissors and glue.

Together they will proceed to cut the paper into small strips and then, with their fingers, make small balls.

Once they have all the balls, they will proceed to assemble a necklace, gluing each of the balls and making a closure at the end.

During the development of the activity, both should work as a team to form the necklace that they are asked, one cuts, the other makes the balls and between the two finish it.

The idea is that they can understand the importance of working not only as a team, but also in confidence, otherwise it would be very difficult to achieve the proposed objective.

GROUP DYNAMICS TO STIMULATE SIMULATION AND IMITATION ACTIVITIES.

37- The mirror

Materials needed for this dynamic: children only

Duration: 30 minutes

Number of children: between 5 and 15 people

ASD children present great difficulty to participate in those activities in which they have to make some representation.

However, by making correct use of the different dynamics, they can learn strategies that contribute to their integration, thus improving their personal relationships.

The children should be placed in pairs, one will be placed in front of the other and should begin to make a series of gestures and signs that the child who observes should imitate.

They can change turns, as they can also change partners, the level of play will advance as the gestures and signs take on a different level of complexity.

The objective is that everyone can participate and become familiar with this type of dynamics that are very often present on a daily basis.

Simulation and imitation activities, not only contribute to fun, but it is a strategy widely used in different contents in the learning process.

38- Guess the message

Materials needed for this dynamic: pencil and paper

Duration: 30 minutes

Number of children: between 5 and 15

The person leading the exercise will divide the participants into small groups and will give each one a sheet of paper and a piece of paper.

Once the information is defined, the children will select a member of the group who will be in charge of transmitting the message to the other children, but without using words.

When he/she comes to the front, he/she will try by all means to explain the assigned message to the group through gestures and signs.

Everyone can participate until they manage to understand the information to be explained.

Once they have deciphered the information, he/she will take his/her place and the other team will go on to make their presentation.

When all participants are ready, a space will be opened to explain the importance of this type of activities, to learn how to manifest and express using representation.

39- Represent the character or object

Materials needed for this dynamic: children only

Duration: 30 minutes

Number of children: between 5 and 15

All the children should make a big circle, and for a few minutes they will have the opportunity to talk about topics of interest, toys, movies, cartoons, food, etc.

After the time has elapsed, some of them will be selected and, depending on the topics discussed, they will start to imitate or represent characters.

They can only give clues, without mentioning the person or thing in specific, everyone can participate, while trying to guess who or what is being represented.

Then the opportunity will be given to another of the children and so on, until they are familiar with the action of pretending or acting out.

Children with ASD are very intelligent and through repetition of activities can achieve meaningful learning.

40- Cuddling

Materials needed for this dynamic: children only

Duration: 30 minutes

Number of children: between 5 and 15

The person who leads the group will explain that they will do a mime activity, dividing them into small teams.

Together they will create several situations, it can be real or imaginary, which will then be represented by themselves through the mimes.

They should try to represent love, friendship, health, suspense, sadness, etc. The intention is that while they represent, they can have a pleasant and fun time.

The children should get together and choose who will be in charge of making the representations.

When all are in agreement, the simulations will be performed, while they participate, the other children will intervene identifying what was the fact that they created and that their classmates are representing.

This type of dynamics for children with ASD are of great relevance, each and every one is focused on trying to solve different problems, however, they are considered integral, because while working one area automatically involves others, yielding positive results.

GROUP DYNAMICS TO WORK WITH IMPULSIVITY

41- Attention to detail

Materials needed for this dynamic: images, drawings of different sizes, photographs.

Duration: 30 – 45 minutes

Number of children: between 5 and 15 people

Children diagnosed with ASD tend to be impulsive, for them, it is very difficult to cope with situations when they experience some kind of discomfort, so often, when frustrated, they may respond with impulsivity.

If they are provided with the appropriate tools, it is very likely that they will learn certain strategies that help them to channel this emotion, thus contributing to improve their interpersonal relationships.

The dynamic consists of forming small groups, in each group, a participant will be selected to start the activity, and after repeating it, the selected participant will take a place in the group to give the possibility to another one to be the protagonist of the experience.

The first child selected is shown a series of images, drawings and photographs, the idea is that he/she can be attentive to every detail, they are shown for a few minutes.

After this time, the images, drawings and photographs are removed and the child is asked about the details and colors observed, the intention is that he/she can reproduce as much as possible everything observed.

This is a dynamic of concentration that helps the child to focus his attention on a specific reality, it is very useful because the child develops the ability to focus his attention on a specific thing to calm down when something is unpleasant and he feels the desire to explode like a volcano.

42- Simon says

Duration: 30 minutes

Number of children: between 5 and 15

The children should be placed in a large circle, one will be selected to be the captain Simon and the one in charge of giving the orders.

The child Simon will start his turn by making a first request "Simon says that everyone must touch their right ear," all children must comply with the request.

Then, gradually changing each request and incorporating a level of complexity, the orders can be faster, repeated or several at a time.

The child who falls behind or does not want to obey will be removed from the game. The last one or ones to reach the end of all the requests will be the winner.

The objective of the activity is to encourage obedience in children, sometimes situations of displeasure often happen in front of parents, representatives, teachers or an adult.

When they intervene in a timely manner, they can prevent children from impulsive behavior in the situation.

If they are oriented to obey before the calls of attention of adults, it will be possible to deal with the facts properly, thus avoiding the uncomfortable moment for the child, as well as for the rest, of an unexpected outburst.

43- Slow motion

Duration: 30 minutes

Number of children: between 5 and 15 people

The children will be placed in a circle in the place where they are, so that the dynamics can be carried out in an orderly and comfortable way.

They will be instructed that, at the beginning of the activity, everyone should start walking in slow motion, as if they were astronauts.

After some time, the signal is changed and they should begin to walk or perform faster activities, such as walking, jogging, jumping.

This dynamic can last as long as it is necessary for them to adapt to follow the instructions.

This activity will help the child to perceive the importance of following instructions, an ideal action for when they are tempted to respond impulsively.

Children with ASD are very intelligent and are able to understand certain instructions and when necessary apply them in their daily lives.

44- The Echo

Duration: 30 minutes

Number of children: 5 to 15 people

The echo represents a very fun activity, which not only provides a significant teaching to the child, but also distracts him/her and leads to the reflection that many times, those things that are so upsetting can be pleasant if they know how to handle them.

On this occasion, the children will have to represent an echo, one child says a phrase and the rest will be in charge of repeating the last syllables.

This last part can be done as a group or one by one they will repeat until the phrase is finished.

This is an activity that requires concentration to be able to perceive what is happening and what should be continued.

And it is precisely there where the greatest emphasis will be made, the situations do not require an immediate response, you always have to carefully observe what is happening and think about the answers that are going to be given in an assertive way.

GROUP DYNAMICS TO WORK ON CREATIVITY

45- Draw the image

Materials needed for this dynamic: sheets of paper, pencils, colors

Duration: 30 minutes

Number of children: between 5 and 15

In general, children with autism tend to be very rigid in their routines, so developing creativity for them is not an easy task.

Dynamics are a fundamental strategy for them to develop their thinking, being able to do motivating activities contribute to open spaces for them to create spontaneously and at the same time provide them with the tools so that they can do it freely in their environment.

The children will be placed in pairs, they will be provided with pencil, paper and colors, the idea is that they can draw their partner, taking into account each and every one of the details that characterize them.

Drawings inspired by their creativity, taking into account references about tastes and interests, among others.

Then it will be the turn of the next partner, once they have finished, they can share their experience with the rest of the group.

If anyone wishes to add something else, they can do so to complement the drawing. This is an activity that apart from developing creative thinking, will be a lot of fun, because everyone will add a special touch to their creation.

As the child is encouraged, he/she can be open to future changes, understanding that not everything is always so square, on the contrary, there are a thousand ways to express ideas that can flow freely when given space.

46- Complete the sentence

Duration: 30 minutes

Number of children: between 5 and 15 people

The children will stand in a circle, the person leading the exercise will create a message and express it out loud.

Example: "Andrea went out to the field," the one next to her should add a new sentence, "Andrea went out to the field in the morning," the next one will add one more, "Andrea went out to the field in the morning to get coffee".

In this way the message will go around in a circle, until it reaches the end, the intention being that the message is not lost.

In case the message gets lost, the child who does not manage to reproduce and complete it must immediately create another one and continue the activity.

Complete the sentence is perfect for working on creativity, since the child will have the immediate need to keep going so as not to lose the thread of the dynamic, concluding it successfully by achieving the objective.

47- Find the exit

Materials needed for this dynamic: sheets of paper and colors

Duration: 30 minutes

Number of children: between 5 and 15 people

A space will be opened for the children to make free drawings and color, while they are doing their activity, the person in charge of carrying out the dynamic will give instructions.

While they are coloring, a fire will be simulated. When they hear "the house is burning," they should get up immediately and look for the exit.

This will be any free space they wish, except that each child must find his or her own way out.

Any child who is left in a pair or group in a space selected by another child will be disqualified.

The dynamic can be repeated several times to stimulate creativity, giving them the possibility to look for or create a different place in each round.

At the end, there is time to share experiences and have fun with the intervention of each partner, which will undoubtedly be unique.

48- Shape it

Materials needed for this dynamic: bond paper and markers

Duration: 30 minutes

Number of children: between 5 and 15 people

The person in charge will tell the children to line up in front of her, who should be located on a wall.

She will stick the bond paper sheet on the wall, select a child from the group and explain to the classmates that they will draw the same child on the paper, but among all of them. If they wish, they can place clothes, shoes, accessories, etc., when they are drawing.

He starts with the shape of the head, and so on, one by one, they will put their features, eyes, nose, mouth, ears, body, arms, trunk, legs and more.

The idea is that everyone can participate, and with their creativity draw their partner as similar as possible.

Being able to contribute new ideas will help them to make an intervention that meets the proposed objective.

The constant use of group activities with children with ASD will facilitate the way for a timely development within each of the contexts in which the child develops.

GROUP DYNAMICS TO WORK ON RULE ADHERENCE

49- Paralyzed

Materials needed for this dynamic: colored cardboard

Duration: 30 minutes

Number of children: 5 to 15 people

Activities to encourage respect for rules cannot be overlooked. Children with ASD find it a conflict to even answer by name when they are called, let alone memorize, assume and comply with a series of orders in relation to something.

When group dynamics are used, tools are provided that allow the development of certain attitudes, among them, the willingness to assume all those rules that are established in specific spaces and moments.

The colored cardboards will be placed on the floor, in the form of a path, indicating the starting point and the arrival point.

One of the children will be selected, who will be in charge of carrying out the activity.

He/she should stand in front of the wall where the arrival point is indicated, the rest of the children will be at the other end waiting for the indications.

The leader child starts counting out loud, while counting, the rest of the children must walk, following the marked line to reach him.

Every so often he/she must count and turn to the group saying "paralyzed", the participants must stop, the leader will observe them, if any of them makes any movement he/she will be disqualified and must withdraw from the dynamics.

This will be done successively until everyone reaches the starting point, the first one will be the winner, but the activity will continue until most of the group can reach the starting point.

This is a very practical way of teaching the need to follow the rules when they are established.

50- The traffic light

Materials needed for this dynamic: poster board, colors and music

Duration: 30 minutes

Number of children: 5 to 15 peple

The traffic light represents a very well known dynamic to manage the subjection to rules.

Any type of activity can be planned, in which the use of the traffic light can be established as limits in the development of the activity.

First, the children are placed in a circle and the meaning of the colors of the traffic light is explained to them: green means to move forward, red means to stop, and yellow means to alert because it is about to change to red.

To do this, the cardboard and the colors are used to draw it so that the children can visualize it.

Then the music will be played and the children will start to dance, the person in charge of carrying out the dynamics will indicate the changes of colors.

When she says "green" everyone will start dancing, when she says "yellow" they must gradually stop dancing and when she says "red," everyone must remain still.

The action is repeated several times, until the children become familiar with the order and each time it becomes easier to obey it.

As long as this type of practice is facilitated, it can be guaranteed that each of these situations that prevent them from adapting easily to the environment, will be worked on and overcome, reaching a better performance in each context.

51- Follow the rule

Materials needed for this dynamic:: sheets of paper, markers, colors, pencils.

Duration: 30 - 45 minutes

Number of children: between 5 and 15 people

The children will be given drawing materials, sheets of paper, markers, pencils, and they will have to start drawing a picture of their preference or related to their interests.

It will be explained to them that even though it is a free expression activity, every time they are given an order, they must obey it in order to continue with the dynamic.

The rules will be very simple, "start the drawing, stop the work and talk for 2 minutes with your partner next to you, exchange the drawing and help your partner with his drawing, exchange colors with the participant behind you, among others.

This is how the activity will go until everyone has finished, the idea is that everyone can focus on the activity under the established parameters, in order to acquire significant learning.

52- Create situations and establish rules

Materials needed for this dynamic: bond paper and markers

Duration: 30 minutes

Number of children: between 5 and 15

Children with ASD have difficulty to assume certain rules, however, they implicitly know them and know that they have to comply with them.

When they do things that are of interest to them, for example, talking or learning about a topic, they do not like to be interrupted, that is one of their rules, as well as many others, it is important to let them know that, just as they like respect for what they do, so do the rest of the people around them.

The children will be asked to create a situation, the one they want, with the exception that, for the development of the same, with guidance, they will have to establish rules.

It can be explaining cooking recipes, something about music, why they choose some favorite toys, among others.

The idea is that while they express themselves they can lead the rest of the group to fulfill all those things they would like to observe in them, while they make their intervention.

Example, "I want you to listen, if you are going to ask or suggest something raise your hand, the interventions of each one will not be able to pass one minute and more."

They will take them and write them on the bond paper and then they will be placed in a visible way so that everyone remembers them.

At the end, they will be asked how they felt and they will be referred to the need to comply with the rules that others establish for them, as it is gratifying that others abide by the limits that each one of them, in their spaces, places.

GROUP DYNAMICS TO WORK ON TOLERANCE

53- Lemons

Materials needed for this dynamic: lemons and a basket

Duration: 20 minutes

Number of children: between 5 and 15 people

Tolerating is a very complex action, we must learn to develop skills to reach agreements with other people, even if they differ from our thoughts, ideas, arguments, others.

The more so for a child with ASD who by nature, his condition makes him live with certain limitations.

This type of activity helps them to develop their thinking, contributing to show tolerance with others, even when their ways and behaviors are not completely understandable.

The children will be placed in a circle and each one will be given a lemon. The basket will be placed in the center of the circle.

The children should take their lemons, observe them carefully and give one or more characteristics of each one of them.

Everyone will have a chance to express themselves, they can exchange ideas with their classmates and complement their own.

Then the lemons will be exchanged among participants, they will observe again and give new characteristics.

At the end of this first part, the person in charge of carrying out the dynamic will tell the children to look for their lemon, they will probably get it without problems, even if some elements are different.

Then this same person will take the lemons and cut them in half, and will tell the children again to look for their lemons, which this time will be more complex, as they will all seem to be the same.

The children are taught that people often seem to be the same, however, they will always have very particular characteristics that make them different, but that, in spite of everything, if there is respect for their ideas, thoughts, expressions, etc., they can enter into any space and develop empathetic relationships with others.

54- The magic circle

Materials needed for this dynamic:: sheets of paper, pencils, basket

Duration: 30 minutes

Number of children: 5 to 15 people

Each child will be given a sheet of paper and a pencil, they will have to select a partner and describe him/her on the sheet, highlighting those characteristics that make his/her personality.

They will take their time and when everyone has finished they will place their paper in the basket that should be in front of them.

Then, by order of the person in charge of leading the dynamic, they will pass one by one, take one of the papers and begin to read.

The rest of the classmates will listen attentively and when they finish, they can participate by trying to guess to whom the characteristics mentioned correspond.

This will be done with all the papers and classmates, then they will be taught, to end the activity, that all people have unique characteristics that make them different from each other and that, even so, we must learn to tolerate them, respect them and accept them as they are.

55- The 9 and the 6

Materials needed for this dynamic: Bond paper, markers and plastic tape.

Duration: 30 minutes

Number of children: between 5 and 15 people

The children will be placed in two rows, one in front of the other, take the bond paper and draw a 9.

The paper has to be placed in the middle of them, so that some see it one way and the others see it another.

The dynamic begins with the participation of everyone, they go in pairs, one is placed in one corner of the paper and the other on the other outside, they must observe and express what they perceive.

The most natural thing will be that the one who observes on one side sees a 9 and the one who observes on the other side sees a 6.

This way they will pass until everyone participates, because it is the same image, the same result will be obtained.

Finally, it should be explained that everyone was right, because from their perspective, some saw a 9 and the other a 6, both were right.

For this reason, it is necessary to learn to respect and be tolerant with others, even when their positions are different from ours, each one expresses according to their capacity of perception.

56- The tolerance list

Materials needed for this dynamic: sheets of bond paper, marker and plastic tape.

Duration: 30 minutes

Number of children: between 5 and 15 people

Each child must have a sheet of bond paper and a marker, with the plastic tape he/she will stick it in a visible space and put his/her name on it.

On each sheet, two columns will be made, one with the things they like and the other with the things they don't like.

At the end, one by one they will have the opportunity to read what they wrote, and then make a general paper in which, according to what they expressed, they will write general lines that can benefit everyone.

Such as, "do not insult, make fun of the other, interrupt while expressing, others, and on the side of the positive column "listen, support each other, share and more."

In this way they will be able to understand that tolerating the actions of others goes hand in hand with respecting each of the differences that everyone possesses.

GROUP DYNAMICS TO WORK ON NON-PRECISE LANGUAGE COMPREHENSION

57- The hat

Materials needed for this dynamic: colored paper hats

Duration: 30 minutes

Number of children: between 5 and 15 people

Children with ASD have great difficulty in understanding expressions that do not go hand in hand with non-precise language.

For this reason, it is very difficult to communicate with them through messages with unknown words, metaphors, clues, among others.

The activities and group dynamics are perfect elements for them to develop their thinking and at the same time their ability to understand non-literal language, thus allowing them to perform better in each of the environments of their daily lives.

The five colored hats will be taken and placed on the table, the colors should be yellow which represents joy, white tranquility, red energy, blue intelligence and black sadness.

Then, five participants should be selected, who will be in charge of making certain representations, using signs and gestures that go according to the color of the hat of their preference.

While the participant makes his or her representation, the rest of the classmates must observe carefully in order to understand what message is being expressed.

If someone discovers it, he/she must stand up, ask permission, go to the front, take the hat that corresponds to the action and put it on.

The same will be done in the same way with the five participants, and then end the dynamic, explaining that not always the information that reaches us will do so clearly and literally.

Many times, it is necessary to learn to discern even intentions to be able to understand, it is not wrong, it is only a form of expression and adapting to them contributes to improve interpersonal relationships.

58- Explain the message in different ways

Materials needed for this dynamic: sheets of paper, pencils, markers, images, others.

Duration: 50 – 60 minutes

Number of children: between 5 and 15

Place all the children in a circle and give them a piece of paper with a message, which they should express to their classmates using metaphors, signs, images, drawings and more.

Each one will read their message carefully and will be given 5 to 10 minutes to create their participation.

They will then be allowed to express the assigned message, but cannot express it using any clear words written on the paper.

On the other hand, the listening group will have a sheet of paper and a pencil in hand with which they can take notes, copying ideas and key words that will allow them to formulate a message with what they want to say.

When everyone has made their participation, then they will proceed to read the same, what they have understood and is similar to the original message, will be the winners of the activity.

At the end of the activity, the participants are told about how necessary it is to be open to the understanding of other forms of communication, being able to understand metaphors, jokes, expressions that are literal helps to relate in a better way in different environments.

59- Tell me what you want

Materials needed for this dynamic: children only

Duration: 30 minutes

Number of children: between 5 and 15 people

Children will be divided into pairs, they will have a few minutes to interact.

They will only use the word "tell me what do you want" at the beginning, it will be done in turn, while one asks, the other must decipher.

In this dynamic, you can not use words, not even metaphors, only signs, it will be a challenge for those who have the turn to understand what you want to tell them.

As it is not so easy for children with ASD to express in this way and even less to understand, they will carry out the activity with the guidance of an adult who will allow them to participate in an effective way, achieving the learning that is to be transmitted.

Surely, it will not be a simple task, but undoubtedly, it will be very fun and meaningful for him.

60- Photos that speak

Materials needed for this dynamic: photographs of different events, magazine clippings, caricatures, others.

Duration: 30 minutes

Number of children: between 5 and 15 people

The pictures that speak is a very practical dynamic to help children with ASD in the comprehension of non-precise language.

The children will be asked to sit in a big circle, the person who is leading the dynamic will take a number of photos, cut-outs, cartoons, images, selected in advance.

They will be shown to the children one by one and they will be asked what they observe in them, characteristics, emotions, what elements they think there are in the photos that transmit a message.

Then they will be taken one by one and it will be explained that, in fact, all of them have a specific meaning that is transmitted just by observing the image.

For this reason, it is necessary to acquire skills, which develop in thinking, thus allowing to improve the ways of understanding, of those information that many times are transmitted and a not precise language is used.

Perhaps, they are more complex to understand, but it is not impossible, with a little effort, it can be achieved.

GROUP DYNAMICS TO WORK ON THE DIFFICULTY OF ESTABLISHING EYE CONTACT WITH THE OTHER PERSON

61- Look and repeat

Materials needed for this dynamic: children only

Duration: 30 – 45 minutes

Number of children: 5 to 15 people

Establishing eye contact with other people is a complex task for children with ASD, they are usually a bit shy, especially in the first encounters, so being very empathetic is not their forte.

Empathy goes hand in hand with the possibility of making a more direct contact, but a series of particular and natural characteristics come into play in these children that make it difficult for them to open up and let themselves be known.

The "look and repeat" dynamic is a great strategy for them to begin to break down erroneous beliefs they may have about themselves, and thus open up scenarios that allow them to establish better relationships and, therefore, communicative processes.

It will be a very fun activity that includes repeating actions, the child with ASD should work with the guidance of an adult who will help him/her to comply with it and achieve the goal.

They should stand one in front of the other, they will be given a reasonable amount of time to share with each other, in order to break the ice.

They can talk about things of interest to both, toys, games, meals and more, the idea is that little by little they will start to trust each other.

Then a space will be opened in which they will have to repeat a few sentences, the person in charge of directing the dynamics will give them some messages on a piece of paper, one will be in charge of reading and the other of repeating.

Then, the other one takes the paper and reads and the one who read first repeats, to carry out the activity, it is necessary to establish an eye contact, the children must reproduce the message they have heard, with the gestures that have accompanied it.

This will allow the child with ASD to develop skills that will teach him/her to make eye contact with other people, it is not a simple task, but by providing the right tools, learning can be achieved.

62- What objects are missing?

Materials needed for this dynamic: objects, colors, toys, buttons, handkerchiefs, candy, etc.

Duration: 30 minutes

Number of children: between 5 and 15 people

Take the different objects that are available to carry out the dynamic and place them on a table, the children will be around them, so that they can visualize and memorize which objects are present.

One of the children is selected and goes to the front, has the task of carefully observing each and every one of the objects that have entered the game.

Then, taking his place, the person in charge of the dynamics will indicate them to place the handkerchief, which each one must have in his hands, over his eyes.

When everyone's eyes are covered, he/she will proceed to remove some of the objects that were on the table and will leave only a few, if he/she prefers, he/she can also remove one, this will make the activity more complex.

Then, tell the children to remove the scarf from their eyes and call back the child who observed the objects to start.

He/she will ask about the missing object(s) on the table, the child will have to remember what he/she observed and identify what is missing if he/she remembers it, the process between the person asking the question should involve a visual process, not only with the objects but also between them.

If the child gets it right, he/she should be rewarded with a candy, take his/her place and the participation is given to another child.

At the end, talk to them about how necessary it is to look at people when they express something, their bodily manifestations, it also speaks for them, a candy is given to each one and the activity is concluded.

63- Observe and copy

Materials needed for this dynamic: acrylic board, sheets of paper, pencils, markers, plastic tape, eraser.

Duration: 30 – 40 minutes

Number of children: between 5 and 15 people

Each child is given a sheet of paper and a pencil, the dynamic is focused on them writing.

In front of them, the acrylic board is placed, which will be used by the person who is going to transmit the message.

This person will be in charge of placing a number of short messages on the board, giving the children a reasonable amount of time to write and then erasing them to place another one.

She will do this repeatedly, with different messages. When she starts, she should explain to the children that they should observe very well what is written, so that they do not make a mistake when copying it on their sheet of paper.

At the end, each child can read what he/she wrote and corroborate if the message is in accordance with what was expressed in each space, if it is missing or if something else was copied.

For this to develop assertively, the children must be very attentive and observe in detail so that they have the minimum margin of error, at the same time, they develop their observation capacity in each circumstance.

64- Follow me

Materials needed for this dynamic: children only

Duration: 30 minutes

Number of children: between 5 and 15

The children will be placed in pairs, and a starting point and an arrival point will be established in the space where they are located.

The dynamic consists of starting from one place to another, but with the help of their partner.

Holding hands, facing each other, staring at each other, without turning to the sides, they must move from one end to the other, until they reach the point of arrival.

When they arrive, they change and when they come back, the child who was leading the way, will be the one to be directed.

When they have done the two routes, they will sit in a circle and a space will be opened to talk, how did they feel, did they feel confident to let themselves be guided while observing their partner, what did they learn from the activity, what did they learn from the activity?

This last question will refer to the importance of eye contact with the other, it is a form of communication, it is a way of transmitting, it is a way of making oneself understood, it is normal and it is very useful in any communicative process.

GROUP DYNAMICS TO WORK ON INTROVERSION

65- Follow the lyrics

Materials needed for this dynamic: music

Duration: 30 minutes

Number of children: between 5 and 15 people

Another of the difficulties of children with ASD that influences their interaction with others is their introversion, this is one of the characteristics that allows identifying their condition.

They are not introverted due to lack of interest in relating to others, but because they do not have the effective tools to do so.

For this reason, through the different dynamics they acquire skills, which little by little will incorporate them into their daily routine more naturally.

The children will be placed in a circle, music will be played and they will have some time to dance, laugh and interact with each other.

After this time, they relax a little and it is explained to them that next, some music will be played again, while it is playing, they will have to sing it, when paused, one of them will raise his/her hand and continue with the lyrics.

The dynamic is repeated several times, so that the children can participate for the most part, singing and having fun while they do it.

If there is a child who wishes to participate and continue the lyrics more than once, he/she can do so, this will help to break the ice and help them gain confidence.

At the end, it should be explained to them that there are occasions when it is necessary to participate and laugh in different ways, this contributes to open ourselves to know and be known, improving interpersonal relationships.

66- Passing the ball

Materials needed for this dynamic: A ball

Duration: 30 minutes

Number of children: between 5 and 15 people

The children should sit in a circle, the ball will be in the hand of the person in charge of the group, who will carry out the dynamic.

The dynamic consists of taking the ball, mentioning one of the participants and talking a little about his or her general characteristics.

Once he/she has finished his/her participation, he/she will take the ball and throw it to the mentioned partner, who, in turn, will select another partner and will do the same, talk a little about all those particularities that characterize him/her and throw the ball again.

This will be done for as long as necessary, all the children must participate.

At the end, they will talk a little with them about how they felt and what they learned from their classmates.

This will allow to strengthen relationships and communication in a more spontaneous way, leaving aside the withdrawal.

67- Role play

Materials needed for this dynamic: children only

Duration: 30 - 45 minutes

Number of children: between 5 and 15 people

The children will be placed in a circle and will be given a reasonable amount of time to share with each other, talk about what they like, toys, food, sports and more.

A space will be opened in which they will be asked what they want to be when they grow up, in relation to professions or trades and they will be allowed to talk some more time.

Then they will be asked to play a little role-playing, and based on what each one expressed, they will create a circumstance that will allow them to represent their role.

It will be like a free game, in which they will be able to show their capabilities and the way they want to be, projecting themselves in a few years.

Following the indications, they will begin to develop their active role in a fun way, but at the same time reflecting on one of their interests.

This activity will allow them to get out of their withdrawal, to see themselves sharing in a pleasant way with others, and as they exercise, it will be much easier to open up to sharing.

68- Create the sentence

Materials needed for this dynamic: sheets of paper and pencils

Duration: 30 minutes

Number of children: between 5 and 15

The children will be placed in pairs, a pencil and a piece of paper will be given to each one, the person in charge of the activity will explain what the activity consists of.

He/she will stand in front of them talking about different topics, all of them will be of interest to attract their attention.

With the exception that every so often he will say a sentence, he will be silent and the children will have to create the sentence that they think fits with what he will be explaining.

At the end, they will have the opportunity, in pairs, to talk about what each one wrote, it will be a great fun time because most likely, the sentences created will not be related to what was really going on if the person went ahead with his participation.

While sharing and laughing, children will have the possibility to open up to the experience, putting aside for a moment the withdrawal that characterizes them.

If the tools are applied assertively, as the child matures, he/she will be able to overcome this limitation to relate in a timely manner.

GROUP DYNAMICS TO WORK ON OBSESSION WITH PARTICULAR OBJECTS OR THINGS

69- What are your interests?

Materials needed for this dynamic: sheets of paper and pencils

Duration: 30 minutes

Number of children: between 5 and 15 people

Excessive interest in certain things and objects is very natural in children with ASD, they love to be able to talk without limits about things that represent great interest for them.

This dynamic is intended to open spaces for sharing in which they have the opportunity to talk with other children, different topics, while understanding that, although something is very interesting, there is always time to be enriched with other things, which can also be of great importance.

The children will be placed in pairs and will be given a reasonable amount of time to talk to each other about everything they like the most.

The person in charge of carrying out the activity should measure the time, monitoring that both pairs participate.

While they listen to their partners, they can take notes of all those things that the partner mentions and that seem pleasant and fun.

At the end of the time, they will go to the front of the group and start the conversation again, emphasizing what they wrote down that they found interesting.

The rest of the group will listen attentively and if the topics expressed seem attractive to them, they will raise their hand and will be able to participate by adding more elements.

At the end, they will talk about how much fun it is to be able to talk about what attracts them and to be able to hear that not only personal interests are important, but also the point of view and what is appealing to others.

70- The plenary

Materials needed for this dynamic: notebook and pencil

Duration: 30 minutes

Number of children: 5 to 15 people

The plenary session is an ideal way to show that there are many important aspects of a topic that can be discussed.

The children will sit in a circle, this time they will assume the roles of managers and trusted personnel of a company.

It will be explained to them that they will simulate a meeting in which they will have to talk about everything related to the company, services, employees, production, finances, etc., and that everyone must participate in order to reach positive agreements.

The meeting begins and the person who directs the dynamics will take the floor, who will represent the head of the company, to locate the children will begin to explain various situations and will ask them what do you think we can do?

This question will be asked with the purpose of awakening in them the desire to talk and participate, after all, it is a game and if there is something they love is to play.

They will be able to talk about anything that comes to mind, the important thing is that they can talk about many things, which is important for what they are representing.

Then a space will be opened to conclude, in this space, the adult who develops the dynamic will collect all the important ideas expressed by the children, will create a conclusion and will close the meeting.

Then, to close the dynamic, the children will talk about how important it is to talk about things that are of interest to them and that there are other very attractive things that also deserve attention.

71- What do I like?

Duration: 30 minutes

Number of children: between 5 and 15 people

The children will be asked to sit in a circle, the idea is to share and talk freely about the things that each one of them likes.

The dynamics will consist of each one taking the floor, saying his or her name and talking a little about what he or she likes the most and explaining why.

For example, I am Luis and I like music because with it I can dance, study, sleep and more.

This is how it will be done with each of the participants, everyone will be able to express themselves and what they are passionate about.

Then they will begin to exchange a little more, the person who takes the dynamics forward will begin to relate what each one said, he will ask Luis, for example, what he likes or dislikes about what is attractive to Pedro.

In this way, it will be explained to them that there is an innumerable amount of things, that even when each one has specific interests, there are always important topics and things that are worth investing time to know.

72- More than one

Materials needed for this dynamic: sheets of paper and pencils

Duration: 30 minutes

Number of children: between 5 and 15 people

With this dynamic, children with ASD will be able to exercise in the development of thinking, which will allow them to understand that within the things that can generate interest, it is always possible to find a range of possibilities.

Each child will be given a sheet of paper and a pencil, and it will be explained to them that they should write down three things they are most passionate about, something they consider to be the most wonderful thing they have seen or known.

This will be a challenge for them, because when children with ASD are passionate about something, they focus all their energy specifically on it, so incorporating more can be complex.

The person leading the dynamic will be able to approach and guide them, in order to find a second and third option.

When the time allotted for this has elapsed, they will have the opportunity to share what they wrote, mentioning each of the options they considered.

After everyone has participated, they will be asked how they felt about having to talk about something other than what really appeals to them.

Once they have expressed themselves, it should be emphasized that this is how day-to-day life is, there are things they are very passionate about, but in order to give them the importance they deserve, it is not necessary to focus all their energy on them.

It is only necessary to establish a balance, which in the end, will bring as consequences great advantages, because it will allow to know and to be enriched with many more subjects.

GROUP DYNAMICS TO WORK ON INTELLIGENCE DEVELOPMENT

73- Memory

Materials needed for this dynamic: pair cards

Duration: 30 minutes

Number of children: between 5 and 15 people

When talking about intelligence in children with ASD, it may vary according to the level of severity of each case.

Some may be very intelligent and others may have greater difficulty in understanding, however, in both cases, the development of certain dynamic activities and games can contribute to increase their intellectual abilities, thus allowing them to acquire significant learning.

Memory is a well-known and simple dynamic that brings great benefits to those who use it as a strategy.

The children will be instructed to group themselves in pairs, then all the cards will be taken and placed on a table face up, so that all the images can be perceived.

They will go to the table in pairs and will observe them one by one, the dynamics will be worked in pairs so that they can help each other and it will be much easier for them to develop it.

Once they have observed all the cards they will return to their place, the person in charge of carrying out the dynamic will take all the cards and place them face down.

The children will then go to the front and begin to discover card by card looking for their partners, when they find them they select them and remove them.

They will do this successively, until they have discovered and removed all of them, when their turn is over, they will sit down and a new pair will come to the front with the same objective.

When everyone is ready, a conversation is held with them to learn about their experiences, how they felt and if they found the activity too complex, in order to encourage them for the next opportunity.

74- Puzzles

Materials needed for this dynamic: puzzles, sheets and pencils

Duration: 30 - 45 minutes

Number of children: between 5 and 15

The children will be divided into groups of four to five people, the idea is that everyone can participate in the development of the activity.

Each one will be given a puzzle that they will have to put together with the help of everyone, they must collaborate and contribute ideas to achieve the objective.

They will also be given a pencil and a sheet of paper, since once they have assembled the puzzle they will have to create a short anecdote related to the image they have found.

After the time has elapsed, the floor will be open for participation, so that everyone can share their experiences.

At first, they will talk about the way in which they put together the puzzle, whether it seemed a complex or simple activity, as well as about the anecdote, how difficult it was to create it.

This will allow them to measure their ability to carry out this type of dynamic, in order to repeat the same activity as many times as necessary.

Remembering that as the child with ASD matures, he/she will be able to adapt in a better way to his/her environment, since many of his/her difficulties, including the capacity of comprehension, have been adequately worked on.

75- Linking words

Materials needed for this dynamic: sheets of paper, pencils and colors

Duration: 30 – 40 minutes

Number of children: between 5 and 15

Each child will be given a sheet of paper, a pencil and colors, and the person in charge of carrying out the activity will be in charge of starting and explaining what the activity consists of.

The person will dictate to the children a long list of words, and they will copy each one on their sheets of paper.

When they finish copying, they will be given some time to read and form sentences by linking words.

Example, one of the words was "strawberry," they should continue the sentence, strawberry is sweet".

Once they have finished completing their list, they will stand in a circle and children who wish to participate will be given the opportunity to do so. In their participation they should read their list with what each one added.

This will allow them to understand the great amount of options that exist to create, since the words were not linked in a unique way, as each one created what he/she thought was the right thing to do, differentiating one from the other.

76- Acquisition of information

Materials needed for this dynamic: pencils, sheets, basket

Duration: 30 minutes

Number of children: between 5 and 15

Each child will be given a sheet of paper and a pencil, and the basket should be placed in front of them, in the place where they are.

On their sheet they should write questions about different topics of interest, games, toys, foods, hobbies, more. Only questions without answers.

When they have finished, they will take their sheets, fold them and put them in the basket in front of them.

Then, one of the children will be chosen to be in charge of drawing each card at random and reading the question.

The child who thinks he/she has the answer will raise his/her hand, stand up and give the appropriate answer to the question that was asked.

If any other child wishes to participate in relation to the same question, to add more information and complement, he/she may do so.

The objective is that everyone can be enriched with their knowledge, thus developing the ability to understand and acquire significant learning.

GROUP DYNAMICS TO WORK ON SELF-ESTEEM

77- How am I?

Materials needed for this dynamic: sheets of paper, pencils, cardboard, colors, scissors, glue, bag.

Duration: 30 minutes

Number of children: between 5 and 15

Sometimes children with ASD show apathy and indifference towards certain things and people, they feel unmotivated and lack self-esteem.

It is something common in them, it is possible that it is related to their weaknesses in the emotional areas.

However, like all the conflicts they usually present, this one can also be worked through the assertive use of group dynamics.

The children will be given pencil, paper, cardboard, colors, scissors and glue, and they will be instructed to write on the paper qualities and nice things that they consider a person should have.

At the end, they will take a scissors, cut out each word separately, fold it and put it in a bag.

Then, they will get into pairs, on the cardboard and the marker, each one will draw the silhouette of their partner on it.

Each one will take his bag. One will start first and take out a paper and read the quality and the other one will have to decide if that quality looks like him, if so, he will take it and with the glue he proceed to paste it on his body drawn on the cardboard.

The one that resembles him/her is glued and the one that does not, is discarded, then it will be the turn of the other teammate, along the same lines.

This dynamic facilitates a good way to get to know the personality, accept it and focus on those positive aspects that each person has and makes him/her unique.

The same is the case for children with ASD, their characteristics and qualities make each one of them a special being, and it is of most importance to let them know it.

78- Motivation glasses

Materials needed for this dynamic: poster board, markers, plastic tape, plastic tape.

Duration: 30 minutes

Number of children: between 5 and 15 people

The children will stand in a circle and a small space will be opened for them to talk about the positive and beautiful things they can see in other people.

After that time, they will proceed to start the dynamic, one by one, they will take the floor and tell their classmates a positive characteristic that they observe in them.

For example, "Luis is very intelligent," "Martha is very creative," "José is super funny," among others. All of the characteristics should speak to a good that each one possesses. This way everyone will have the opportunity to participate.

At the end, take the poster board and markers, place it with plastic tape in a visible place in front of them and write down all the wonderful characteristics that everyone mentioned.

Once they have written them all down, they will read them aloud and hug each other as a sign of congratulations for possessing qualities that make them unique and allow them to relate empathetically with others.

79- The statues of emotions

Materials needed for this dynamic: children only

Duration: 30 minutes

Number of children: 5 to 15

The children will be divided into two equal groups, each group will be placed in a circle next to each other.

When the music stops, the first group should remain as statues reflecting an emotion.

On the other hand, the second group will approach them to observe them and guess what emotion it is. For example, smiling faces, surprises, admiration, among others.

The music continues to play and the activity is repeated, this time it is group two that remains as statues and group one that must guess.

The same activity can be repeated as many times as the person who directs the dynamic considers it necessary, then the activity ends and a comfortable conversation takes place in which everyone can express the positive and fun things they observed in their classmates.

This will lead them to reflect that this is how all human beings are, they have characteristics that allow them to cheer up and motivate people, whenever they need it, that makes them important in their lives.

80- Challenge

Materials needed for this dynamic: colored chalk, drawings

Duration: 30 - 45 minutes

Number of children: between 5 and 15

The person in charge of carrying out the dynamic should establish several challenges with the children, create a story in five minutes, sing a song, color a drawing made on cardboard beforehand, etc.

The person in charge of carrying out the dynamic should establish several challenges with the children, create a story in five minutes, sing a song, color a drawing made on cardboard beforehand, etc.

He/she will give each child a number that identifies him/her and with which he/she will take his/her place when it corresponds to him/her.

Then, with the colored chalk, draw on the floor several squares that must be identified with the name of the challenges that were established.

He will then proceed to select a child at random, who will have to come to the front and select the square with the challenge he wants to perform.

Once located, he can choose the classmates he wants to help him meet the challenge, these will be the five above or below his number.

For example, if he has the number six, he should select 5,4,3,2,1, or 7,8,9,10,11.

The children mentioned above will come to the front, place themselves with him in the box and begin to perform the challenge.

At the end, they will take their place and the person in charge of carrying out the dynamic may select another child at random to perform another challenge. The rules will be the same and the idea is that everyone participates.

Once this time is over, everyone will stand in a circle and share their experience about how they felt during the activity.

Emphasis should be placed on how important everyone is, with their strengths, to achieve the proposed objectives.

GROUP DYNAMICS FOR WORKING ON SENSITIVITY TO DIFFERENT SENSORY STIMULI

81- Color game

Materials needed for this dynamic: colored cardboard and scissors.

Duration: 30 – 45 minutes

Number of children: between 5 and 15 people

Children who are diagnosed with ASD present certain sensitivity to different sensory stimuli, for this reason, it is necessary to provide them with tools that allow them to exercise control over their actions when exposed to this type of situations.

The children will sit in small groups, take the cards and cut them into squares, which should have, by color, the same amount. That is, 4 green, 4 red, 4 yellow, 4 white, 4 blue and so on.

Once all the squares are ready, they will sit around the table and per group they will place a color card, everyone must observe carefully, the first member to notice that all the cards of the same color are on the table, must shout "color game."

The game will continue until all the cards are on the table, the group with the most correct guesses will be the winner.

Then open a space for conversation, they are allowed to talk about their experience while participating with the desire to win.

This type of dynamics allows us to develop the ability to fix our concentration on something important when we want something.

In the same way it happens when an event around is extremely disturbing, to remove the attention is the best way to reach peace in situations that usually alter it.

82- The castle

Materials needed for this dynamic: wooden blocks

Duration: 30 minutes

Number of children: between 5 and 15

The person in charge of carrying out the exercise will divide the children into two equal groups.

A table will be placed in between them, where they will have to start building a castle with the wooden blocks.

All the members of the group must participate and work on the construction of the castle. If when one of them places the block the castle falls down, the round will be lost and all the teams will have to start the activity again.

This activity requires a lot of concentration, since a small oversight will start the dynamic from scratch and a lot of time will be lost to achieve the goal.

In the same way it happens with those events that can be disconcerting, taking the attention away from them is the best way to continue the routines, without adverse situations disturbing more than necessary.

83- Read carefully

Materials needed for this dynamic: story and music

Duration: 30 minutes

Number of children: between 5 and 15 people

Each child will take a story and choose a place where he/she wants to read it in the space where they are.

The person in charge of the dynamic will play music at a low volume, then instruct the children to start reading.

While they read, little by little the music will increase in volume, they cannot stop reading, if there is something they get lost in, they must go back to the music to understand.

This is how the dynamics will continue for as long as the person directing it considers necessary.

Then he/she will indicate that the reading should be stopped, and will initiate a time to listen to what each one understood from the reading.

In addition, they should express how the high volume may have affected them and how they managed to continue with the activity.

Emphasizing that it is possible to concentrate all the attention on something that really generates peace, when those annoying situations appear.

84- Look carefully

Materials needed for this dynamic: sheet of bond paper, colored markers, plastic tape.

Duration: 30 minutes

Number of children: between 5 and 15 people

The children will be placed in pairs and will be given a sheet of bond paper, markers and plastic tape.

Together they will have to write a series of words and numbers on it, once they have finished they will have 10 minutes to memorize all the details.

At the end of this time, they will proceed to make their presentation and present from memory what they remember most of what they have written.

This is an activity that requires concentration because, even if they create their own poster, it may be difficult to repeat what they have done without looking at it.

These concentration activities allow them to develop skills that lead them to distract their attention from those sensory stimuli that can destabilize them, allowing them to develop in their contexts with greater freedom.

GROUP DYNAMICS TO WORK ON THE ABILITY TO ACCEPT THE AFFECTION AND SUPPORT OF OTHERS

85- I support you

Materials needed for this dynamic: sheets of paper, colors, cardboard, pencils, music.

Duration: 30 – 45 minutes

Number of children: between 5 and 15 people

It is very difficult for children with ASD to accept affection and expressions of support from others.

Precisely because they are so withdrawn, this is a very difficult task for them. However, providing them with tools helps them to learn about affection towards others, as well as to receive the affection they wish to show to them.

The children will be placed in pairs, they will be instructed to develop a task, it can be painting, drawing, singing, dancing, among others.

Then they will be given a specific time to develop it, sometimes, when a joint work is assigned, there is one who takes the lead and wants to take control of the activity.

In this case it should be done calmly, because both must work on the realization of what is assigned, coloring, drawing, singing, creating and more, can be complex, but not impossible. It will allow the child or children with ASD to observe and practice that working with the help and support of the other is meaningful.

86- Let's build together

Materials needed for this dynamic: cardboard, sheets of paper, colors, markers, scissors, glue, plasticine, figures.

Duration: 30 – 45 minutes

Number of children: between 5 and 15 people

The person in charge of carrying out the activity will form small groups with the children and will give them the material and assign them the activity.

Each group will be given, apart from the materials, some figures, which both groups will have to build.

At the end of the activity, they should explain to the other children how the construction process went and how useful their participation was.

At the end, they should talk about the importance of being receptive to the help and support that others are willing to give.

There are circumstances in life in which one cannot carry out a task alone, and necessarily requires the intervention of the other, even in the simplest tasks to be performed.

It must be internalized, that opening up, does not mean danger, on the contrary, "with support, it can be achieved".

87- Who am I?

Materials needed for this dynamic: sheets of paper and pencils

Duration: 30 minutes

Number of children: between 5 and 15 people

The children will sit in a circle, all with a sheet of paper and a pencil, on which they should take note of the interventions of their classmates.

Each one will have the right to speak and will talk about the nice characteristics that they themselves have, everyone will listen and take notes, they should not mention anyone specifically, only in a general way.

When they have finished their participation, they will choose a partner and give him/her some of the characteristics that were mentioned between all of them.

For example, "Marcos I choose you because I think you are caring, kind, applied, intelligent, take these words, I give them to you."

The partner mentioned should choose another, "Luisa I choose you because I think you are loving, good companion and kind, take these words, I give them to you."

In this way they will be mentioned one by one, until all have expressed themselves and have their words.

A small conversation will be held at the end, in which reference will be made to the importance that each person has for the others, which is why they always want to show their affection and support as many times as necessary.

88- Hugs

Materials needed for this dynamic: children only

Duration: 30 minutes

Number of children: between 5 and 15 people

The children will be placed in a circle and will be given a short time to talk and share with each other about the things they like the most, in order to break the ice and build trust.

After that time, the person in charge of carrying out the dynamics will indicate that they will make a brief presentation, nothing to worry about, because everyone will be able to speak freely, since the topic will be chosen by all of them.

In addition, after the excellent participation of each one, the prize will be a big hug.

The particularity is that after the child finishes speaking, he/she will choose who will give him/her the prize, since, once he/she gives him/her a hug, he/she will take the floor again and will present his/her presentation.

It will be a very amusing activity, since it will allow to strengthen the bonds of trust and fraternal affection among all, thus developing the ability to understand how pleasant is the manifestation of affection on the part of the other.

GROUP DYNAMICS TO WORK ON THE DIFFICULTY OF REPEATING PHRASES, WORDS OR SOUNDS IN A CONSECUTIVE WAY

89- Repeating

Materials needed for this dynamic: bond paper or acrylic board and markers.

Duration: 30 minutes

Number of children: between 5 and 15 people

Being able to repeat certain phrases, words or sounds becomes a challenge for children with ASD.

They tend to use a very structured language, so repetition is not their forte, which is known as echolalia.

Facilitating some tools, this difficulty can be worked successfully allowing the child to incorporate without major inconvenience to the activities that require this type of exercise.

The person in charge of carrying out the dynamics, will work with the children in certain areas of learning, at first it can be language and mathematics, based on letters, sentences and numbers.

All the information will be copied on a sheet of bond paper or on the blackboard and then the exercise will begin.

The exercise will consist of repetition, first they will have to repeat the information that the guiding adult indicates and then a child will be selected at random to take the place and direct them, this action can be repeated several times.

This is a very simple and well-known dynamic and learning technique, which will allow them not only to develop the expected skill, but also the ability to memorize.

For this reason the importance of group dynamics. Not only help with one aspect, with their application many more are covered.

90- Imitates sound

Materials needed for this dynamic:: children only

Duration: 30 – 45 minutes

Number of children: between 5 and 15 people

All children will make a big circle, a communicative process will start in which they will freely express their likes and dislikes about pets.

In general, children are pet lovers and are always attracted to anything related to pets.

After a while, in the same circle, they will sit down to talk, now, in front of everyone, about those animals they have at home or with which they have shared at some point.

One by one they will mention the pet of their preference, give its characteristics, explain why they like it and the funniest thing is that they will have to imitate its sound.

This dynamic is extremely fun, because while the children are talking and expressing the different sounds, it is very likely that, for the rest, it will be very funny.

Then, at the end, while laughing, the children will be told that rigidity in language should often be left aside, in order to be able to express with greater freedom and practicality the information that is to be transmitted.

91- Sing with me

Materials needed for this dynamic: children only

Duration: 30 minutes

Number of children: between 5 and 15 people

The group leader will put the children in pairs, so that they can work together and achieve the objective more easily.

They will have to choose a song that they both like and that they can sing together, they must know the lyrics or most of it.

The dynamics will consist in that at the order of the person who carries out the dynamics, they will have to start singing the song, but in parts.

That is to say, one starts with the verse, keeps silent, the other continues with the chorus, both repeat it, if there is any part that they do not know then they must imitate the lyrics and music by making sounds, in this way until the end of the song.

Everyone will have the opportunity to make their presentation, and then, at the end, collect the experience of each one.

Formal language is very useful in many of the daily routines, but getting out of it and expressing oneself in a spontaneous and even funny way is also necessary in some opportunities.

92- Conveys the message

Duration: 30 minutes

Number of children: between 5 and 15 people

The children will be placed in a circle, the person who performs the dynamic will be to deliver several messages.

He/she will choose a few children to reproduce them to the rest, but with the exception that the children will have to use not only words but also sounds.

For example, "Pedro will be in charge of explaining to the group that Maria will not be able to play because she is sick and they took her to the hospital to give her an injection, the poor thing cried her eyes out".

As well as this, different messages will be given, the children chosen, will then have the responsibility to express them to the group following the rules explained.

At the end, they will be able to share their experience and emotions that arose during the activity, emphasizing the importance of acquiring skills in the different forms of expression.

Being able to repeat phrases, sounds, words and more is part of many of the activities that are developed on a daily basis.

GROUP DYNAMICS TO WORK ON THE DEVELOPMENT OF SKILLS TO GIVE ASSERTIVE ANSWERS TO THE QUESTIONS ASKED

93- What question?

Materials needed for this dynamic: sheets of paper and pencils

Duration: 30 – 45 minutes

Number of children: between 5 and 15

Questions about certain issues are part of every person's daily life.

However, for children who have been diagnosed with ASD it is very complex to give assertive answers when they are asked a question.

The situation, apart from being related to their condition, is also linked to other characteristics that contribute to the increase of this inability, one of them is the lack of concentration.

Making use of relevant group dynamics collaborates in helping them, so that, if they can pay a little more attention to listen well and process the information, they will then be able to answer each question correctly or at least get close to them.

The person in charge of carrying out the dynamic will tell the children to stand in a circle.

He will walk among them and tell them that he wants to hear them talk a little about their likes and interests.

Each one will take the floor and begin to express themselves freely, being something that interests them, surely, it will not be very difficult.

Then, a space for questions and answers will be opened, the same will be done according to what each one expressed, the leader will emphasize that they must listen well to be able to answer correctly.

In case of not understanding or not knowing how to answer, the child should then say "What question? To explain, rephrase it or otherwise give them more time to think, this will contribute to their understanding and therefore to a more assertive response.

94- The debate

Materials needed for this dynamic: sheets of paper and pencils

Duration: 30 - 45 minutes

Number of children: between 5 and 15

The children will be divided into two equal groups, they will be given a small but opportune time to talk to each other.

In the middle of this interaction they should choose a topic that they are all passionate about, a topic they can talk about without the need to read or do research on the spot. Then they will proceed to formulate some questions related to that topic.

When they have everything ready, then they will place one group in front of the other, one of them starts the activity, will ask a question that both groups planned, the member of the opposite team who knows the answer, will raise his hand and answer.

They also have the option of asking for time, joining together, answering and choosing who will speak for everyone.

Then it is the next group's turn to ask and the other group's turn to answer.

In this way, several exchanges will take place, depending on the questions that are elaborated, the team with the most correct answers wins.

Debate is a very popular group dynamic used to discuss any topic, thus generating significant learning.

95- The interview

Materials needed for this dynamic: sheets of paper and pencils

Duration: 30 – 45 minutes

Number of children: between 5 and 15 people

The children will be placed in pairs, all of them, with their partner, will have to simulate an interview.

They will choose an action, the one they like, it can be real or imaginary, and they will plan how to represent it.

It can be a visit to the doctor, important characters, eating contests, the best games and toys, among others.

They will write a series of questions and then organize themselves by choosing who is the interviewer and who responds as they simulate their scene.

Each pair will have their chance to participate, enriching the others, not only with their content, but also with the ability to give timely answers to what is being asked.

96- How many are there?

Materials needed for this dynamic: sheets, pencils, colors, buttons, toys and different small objects.

Duration: 30 - 45 minutes

Number of children: between 5 and 15 people

The person in charge of carrying out the exercise will organize the children in small groups.

In the center of the space, place as many objects as possible in a disorderly manner, the teams will have the task of collecting them one by one and organize them according to their category and quantity, as some of them will be repeated.

For example, if they organize the toys, they must specify: 5 toys, one car, two dolls, one ball, 10 colors, one red, one blue, one red, one blue, one red, one blue, one red, one blue.

10 colors, one red, one blue, one purple, three yellow, two black, two white, and so on with all the objects.

Once organized, the facilitator will ask group by group what they ordered, quantities and colors.

Everyone will have the opportunity to participate and respond, until a complete record of what each group did is available.

The closed and precise questions, also help to a better understanding of them, giving the possibility to children with ASD, in the midst of their difficulty to respond according to what is being asked.

GROUP DYNAMICS TO WORK ON ANGER

97- Free yourself from anger

Materials needed for this dynamic: sheets of paper, pencils, balloons

Duration: 30 – 45 minutes

Number of children: between 5 and 15 people

Children with ASD are characterized by being very impulsive in certain situations, they respond and intervene in an exaggerated way, without being able to exert their own control over their actions.

One of their most common impulses is anger attacks, when they feel pressured or frustrated by something that is beyond their understanding, they tend to explode in the environment in which they find themselves.

Therefore, from a very young age, we work with them through different games and dynamics that allow them to channel this emotion in the best possible way.

The children will be given a sheet of paper, a pencil and a balloon, on which they will have to write those things that irritate them so much and that every time they have to face them, they end up exploding in anger.

They will have a prudential time so that they can think and express themselves freely.

Once they have finished, they will take their paper, fold it and introduce it into the balloon, filling it with air. Then, they will go outside and make it fly, calling it the balloon of rage.

When returning to the space, it should be explained to them that many times there are situations that escape from their hands and it is not possible to solve, at least not instantly, but that the explosions of anger are very harmful, they weaken and make the body sick.

For this reason, it is best to talk about what bothers, calmly and let it go, at some point, you can resume and give timely responses, the ultimate goal of every human being, should always be feel good.

98- The glass of water

Materials needed for this dynamic: glasses, jugs with water, tables, music.

Duration: 30 – 45 minutes

Number of children: between 5 and 15 people

The activity begins with a free conversation with the children, addressing the topic of anger, but giving them the freedom to express themselves spontaneously, what bothers them the most? Why? What do they feel when they explode in anger and afterwards? These are some of the questions that can be used to guide the interaction of the moment.

Then the table is set up, the children will be standing around it, in front of them will be a glass and a pitcher with water, one for each, next to it one or two spare glasses.

In the background music will play. The dynamic guide will explain that while the music plays, they must gradually fill the glass. When everything is silent they will stop, while the music plays they must fill, they cannot stop. This must be done several times, while they fulfill the task.

However, omit that there will come a time when the music will not stop, but will continue to play, that is where they will have to deal with the complexity, because they will have to use the spare glasses, but when finished, if the music continues to play they will have no choice but to let the water over the last glass.

When observes that the children are spilling the water, it will be necessary stop the music a give a new glass to each one and indicate that they must collect all the water in it.

Surely, for the children this order will cause an impact or impression, since it is an impossible task, then the adult will take place and will sit them in a circle and proceed to explain to them that this way, just as it happened with the water, it happens when they give place to the explosions of anger.

Once you explode and act inappropriately, it is very difficult to pick up and explain why you reacted in that way, for that reason, in these situations, it is best to take a deep breath, find a space to relax and let it go, there will be time to seek solutions.

99- The volcano

Materials needed for this dynamic: sheets of paper, pencils and colors

Duration: 30 – 45 minutes

Number of children: 5 to 15 people

The children will be given a sheet of paper, pencils and colors. The guide will talk with them about the activity of the volcano, the lava begins to boil, until it erupts, causing it to explode and producing a disaster.

Then a comparison is made with the outbursts of anger, the floor is given to them so that they can participate, and they are asked how the volcano can be related to anger? How are they similar? What are the elements that can be compared?

Once everyone has participated, you will explain that yes, anger is really like a volcano, when the person is about to explode, he/she begins to feel a little heat in the bottom of his/her stomach or as if something is stirring and wants to come out.

But unlike the volcano, human beings are able to stop the eruption and therefore the disaster, when you start to feel that the volcano wants to explode, you have to take action, go out, breathe, focus your attention on something else, until the discomfort begins to subside.

Finally, they are asked to draw a volcano, put their name on it and write down the possible actions to take when they find themselves in a situation that causes them irritation.

100- The Monster

Materials needed for this dynamic: sheets of paper, pencils, colors, jar with lid.

Duration: 30 - 45 minutes

Number of children: 5 to 15 people

Start the dynamic by talking with the children about anger, giving them the opportunity to express themselves and talk about all those things that destabilize them.

The children are asked how they think those annoying impulses can be identified and with what, a tsunami, an earthquake, a monster, among others, guiding them to choose a monster.

Then they are given the paper, pencils and colors and are asked to draw this horrendous monster called anger and do not forget to put their respective face, eyes, nose, mouth and of course, to the paper, the name of each one, they are asked to color it, after all if it is their monster it must be pretty.

When everyone has finished their drawing, they will take it, fold it and put it in the jar, closing it with its lid very tightly.

It will be explained to them that each one's monster has been locked up and that the only way it can come out is if they themselves take it out again.

For that reason, when you find yourself in a situation where you feel anger and want to explode impulsively, remember that the monster was destroyed and imprisoned and that, if you let it out, you will then have to catch it again in order to imprison it.

The best and most practical thing to do is to think, breathe, leave and then, in a serene manner, take up the situation again to find possible solutions.

GROUP DYNAMICS FOR WORKING ON UNDERSTANDING THE LIMITS OF PERSONAL SPACE

101- From your place

Materials needed for this dynamic: small objects, colored chalk, table.

Duration: 30 – 45 minutes

Number of children: 5 to 15 people

It is well known that children who develop autism have a hard time respecting each other's personal space.

Many times their hyperactivity leads them to not know that there are limits and that these must be respected.

There are many activities that help them to become aware of, know and respect what is part of the individuality of others, thus allowing them to establish better interpersonal relationships.

The person who guides the dynamic will organize the children in small groups, and with the colored chalk will mark out the space on the floor to carry out the dynamic.

First, he/she will place from end to end, a starting point and an end point, between each point he/she will establish several lines, according to the group of organized children and in them several circles, with a prudential distance, which will be the bridge between the starting point and the end point, in the starting point a table with small objects will be placed.

Then each child, by group, according to the row that corresponds to them, will be placed in the circles, others, representatives of their group will be at the table and they will be in charge of passing the objects.

The objects must pass through all the hands until they reach the starting point. No child may leave his circle, nor try to be closer to the other, much less touch the space of his partner.

If it is difficult to pass the object, they must find a way to do it, respecting the rules. The team that manages to pass the most objects will be the winner.

102- Solve

Materials needed for this dynamic: sheets of bond paper, markers and plastic tape.

Duration: 30 - 45 minutes

Number of children: between 5 and 15 people

The children will have the challenge of solving certain activities assigned by the guide, with the particularity that each one will do it from their own space, respecting that of the others.

The bond paper sheets will be placed on the wall, one sheet will be divided in two, and two children will work on it, not in pairs, individually, but on the same sheet, one half for each one.

The activities are assigned by the person in charge of the dynamic.

The activities will range from copying words, solving mathematical exercises, giving answers to questions and riddles and more.

For everything they will have a limited time, it is not allowed to say to the partner, permission, make room for me, move a little, among others, they must work in silence, from their small space.

Then, they will be placed in a circle in order to talk a little about their experience, how they felt and what is the significant learning that it leaves them.

103- Change

Materials needed for this dynamic: music and colored chalk

Duration: 30 minutes

Number of children: between 5 and 15 people

The children will be organized in pairs, and with the colored chalk, a space will be delimited for each pair, making a circle or square on the floor.

The dynamic consists in that everyone, with their partner, will begin to dance inside the circle in which they were placed, when the guide indicates "change," they must quickly move to the space of the partner on the right side.

They cannot stay outside of any circle, nor in the one they were in, they must move, and continue the dance, respecting each space.

The order will be given a few times, until the guide concludes the activity, so that then, there will be a time of sharing, in which they can express their experience, and how complex or simple it can be, even in the simplest things, to respect the space of others.

104- Wait your turn

Duration: 30 minutes

Number of children: between 5 and 15 people

All children will sit in a circle, listening to the voice of their guide, they will be given a space to interact freely among them, these times are usually very important because it helps to break the ice, if there is any.

Then they will begin the activity, they will start talking about topics of interest to the children, the leader will ask questions and the children will have to raise their hands and wait their turn to answer.

The activity will become a little more complex when the guide begins to make interventions, depending on what the children say, but with intention, changing data and information.

Probably the children will be tempted to interrupt to correct him, however, under his command "wait your turn," they must remain calm and understand that they must wait their turn.

At the end, they will close with a small reflection on the importance of respecting the space of others and knowing how to wait their turn to participate in them, only if they are allowed to, this is part of a good coexistence.

GROUP DYNAMICS TO WORK ON THE NEED TO BE ALONE

105- Join me

Materials needed for this dynamic: children only

Duration: 30 minutes

Number of children: between 5 and 15 people

The conflict to establish interpersonal relationships is one of the main and general characteristics of the autistic spectrum.

But it is not only about improving their relationships of trust, empathy, sharing with others to integrate them in the best way, it is also about helping them to overcome that permanent desire of wanting to be alone, and that is precisely the objective that is pursued, through the different dynamics and games that are used as strategies.

The children will sit in a circle, the person in charge of the dynamic will assign them a simple task, write a poem, read a reading, create a simulation, sing a song, among others.

They will proceed to choose, among the children, with whom they want to work, in this opportunity, pairs will not be assigned, but they will freely decide.

But before making their choice, they will express, to their partner, a nice and positive characteristic, example, "Andrea, you are very bright, come with me to work."

In this way, they will do it all, until they are located and can take a space to fulfill the assigned task.

The objective is that apart from encouraging teamwork, everyone can feel loved and useful by all their peers, this will allow them to open up to working together in future meetings.

106- Creating

Materials needed for this dynamic: sheets of paper, pencils, markers, plastiline, paint and more.

Duration: 30 – 45 minutes

Number of children: between 5 and 15

It is well known that both being accompanied and creating are not part of the strengths of a child with ASD.

However, when the different strategies are used in the right way, they always bring about significant learning.

The person who carries out the dynamic will tell the children to form small groups, choosing the partners with whom they want to work.

This dynamic enjoys freedom, because the children will create according to their tastes and interests, they will paint, write, recite, dance, among other activities.

They will be given the materials and get to work. Once they have finished their tasks, they will have a time to expose the work they did and how they did it together, that is, what each one did, showing the important participation of all classmates.

The fact that they can create, according to their tastes and interests, is a strategy to capture the attention of children with ASD, so that they feel the need to work in company.

107- Sharing

Materials needed for this dynamic: sheets of paper, pencils and colors

Duration: 30 - 45 minutes

Number of children: between 5 and 15 people

The children will be given their materials to work with, sheets of paper and pencils. The colors will be given to some of them and not to others, with the proviso that all of them must color, so they will be of general use.

Each child will be given a drawing to do, a landscape, a beach, a mountain, different animals, roses, trees, others, and a certain time will be given to complete the task.

The activity begins and everyone will begin to draw. Exactly when it is time to paint, will lead to the objective pursued, and is that children can't finish the job alone, they must necessarily seek the company and collaboration of their partners to finish.

Once they finish and are congratulated for their excellent work, it should also be emphasized how necessary and indispensable it is for every human being to be surrounded by great people in different opportunities.

108- Take my hand

Materials needed for this dynamic: children only

Duration: 30 - 45 minutes

Number of children: between 5 and 15 people

The children will be asked to sit in a circle and the person leading the exercise will start with a short reflection on the importance of other people in their lives.

He/she will also tell them that all human beings, without exception, always need to be with someone to talk, talk, play, laugh, among others.

When he finishes his intervention, he will give the floor to the children and ask their opinion about loneliness, their fears, dislikes, other people and more.

Once everyone has participated, they will be numbered 1 and 2, and so on, until everyone is identified.

Then divide them into two groups, group 1 and group 2, both should make a simulation related to an action that represents help to others, while making their representation should include the phrase "take my hand," giving a closure to the same successful.

For example, if they simulate that someone falls, they should offer help to pick them up, if they simulate that someone is hungry, they should offer food to help them, in this way in any action that is represented.

When everyone has finished, it will be emphasized to them that this is how day to day life is, we all need the other and the other needs us, there is no reason to isolate ourselves when there are so many wonderful people around us.

GROUP DYNAMICS TO WORK ON THE USE OF THE DIFFERENT MEANS OF COMMUNICATION IN AN APPROPRIATE WAY

109- The message

Duration: 30 – 45 minutes

Number of children: between 5 and 15

The correct use of all means of communication is fundamental for a good development in the environment.

Children with autism lack these skills, which, together with other weaknesses, make their situation much more complex for an effective integration in each of their contexts.

First, make a big circle with all the children present. The person who guides them will be in charge of carrying out the dynamics.

On small pieces of paper he/she will write a message, which will be given to each child, once they have it in hand they will have the task of transmitting it to the other, using different means, a telephone, a letter, a letter, a mail, among others. Everything must be done through a simulation.

For example, the one who wants to use the telephone should simulate that he/she has one in hand and will give his/her message, the one who decides to use the mail will simulate that he/she is in front of a computer and will give his/her message, and so on with all the messages until they have expressed themselves.

Then, they will be explained the importance of handling the means of communication correctly so that the communication is always effective.

110- Drawing I learn

Materials needed for this dynamic: pencils, sheets of paper, colors

Duration: 30 – 45 minutes

Number of children: between 5 and 15 people

The children will sit in pairs, the dynamic guide will make a brief presentation about the different means of communication that exist to communicate.

They will be able to talk about the different technological media and the use they make of them, explaining why they think they are important, what would happen if they did not exist and more.

The objective is for them to give free rein to their imagination, assuming how useful they really are in everyday life.

Once the conversation is over, they will be given materials, sheets of paper, pencils and colors, and they will be asked to draw the means of communication they know and like best.

When they have finished, they should explain why they like it so much and the specific importance of that medium.

The dynamic of repeating the information is done with the purpose of reinforcing the content covered, allowing them to acquire significant learning.

111- The Letter

Materials needed for this dynamic: sheets of paper and pencils

Duration: 30 – 45 minutes

Number of children: 5 to 15 people

The children will be given a sheet of paper and a pencil and it will be explained to them that they should write a letter of good wishes, emphasizing that the letter or correspondence is part of a means of communication that never goes out of fashion, even when technological advances present new possibilities.

Each child should be inspired and begin to write, the letter should be beautiful, after all, good wishes set the tone.

Once finished, they will proceed to make a circle. The one who guides the dynamics will ask them to choose one of their partners to whom they want to deliver their good wishes.

When everyone has chosen and delivered their letters, then one by one they will proceed to read it, closing the activity with a fraternal embrace explaining again the importance and usefulness of the letter as an effective means of communication.

115- How do you feel?

Materials needed for this dynamic: music

Duration: 30 – 45 minutes

Number of children: between 5 and 15 people

This type of dynamic is related to a relaxation technique. Each child will be asked to place him/herself in the place he/she prefers, a chair, a piece of furniture, the floor, a corner, so that he/she can be comfortable during the development of the dynamic. A very soft music will be chosen and played in the background.

The person who carries out the activity will start it by doing a simple breathing exercise, with eyes closed, inhale and exhale, so that the children are completely calm.

Then he/she will take them to think a little bit about all the beautiful things that happen to them and that they like, their family, friends, games, studies, walks, toys among others.

In order to make room for those things that are not so nice, make them sad and fill them with annoyance, to the point that they want to attack themselves.

When you get there, ask how do you feel? Many will say, annoyed, sad, lonely, apathetic, indifferent.

It is the moment then to offer them strategies, how about imagining? A landscape, a beach, a meal, a mountain, a fun game, among others.

Ask again, did they imagine it, is it beautiful? Then begin the closing with a small reflection, as should be done when anger or frustration drives them to aggression.

Thinking about the beautiful and pleasant things is the best way to change the panorama, there are things that simply escape from your hands and cannot be achieved, and that is not bad, it is just a small part of everyday life, nobody is to blame, except your body, love it and respect it.

Printed in Great Britain
by Amazon